D0774007

Cisco Networking Academy Program
IT Essentials II: Networking Operating Systems
Lab Companion

Cisco Systems, Inc.
Cisco Networking Academy Program

UXBRIDGE COLLEGE
LEARNING CENTRE

Cisco Press

201 West 103rd Street
Indianapolis, IN 46290 USA

Cisco Networking Academy Program
IT Essentials II: Network Operating Systems Lab Companion

Cisco Systems, Inc.
Cisco Networking Academy Program

Course Sponsored by Hewlett-Packard Company

Copyright © 2003 Cisco Systems, Inc.

Published by:
Cisco Press
210 West 103rd Street
Indianapolis, IN 46290 USA

All rights reserved. No part of this book may be reproduced or transmitted in any form or by any means electronic or mechanical, including photocopying, recording, or by any information storage and retrieval system, without written permission from the publisher, except for the inclusion of brief quotations in a review.

Printed in the United States of America   1 2 3 4 5 6 7 8 9 0

First Printing   February 2003

ISBN: 1-58713-096-3

Warning and Disclaimer

This book is designed to provide information about PC and Hardware setup, configuration, and troubleshooting. Every effort has been made to make this book as complete and as accurate as possible, but no warranty or fitness is implied.

The information is provided on an "as is" basis. The author, Cisco Press, and Cisco Systems, Inc. shall have neither liability nor responsibility to any person or entity with respect to any loss or damages arising from the information contained in this book or from the use of the programs that may accompany it.

The opinions expressed in this book belong to the author and are not necessarily those of Cisco Systems, Inc.

This book is part of the Cisco Networking Academy™ Program series from Cisco Press. The products in this series support and complement the Cisco Networking Academy Program curriculum. If you are using this book outside the Networking Academy program, then you are not preparing with a Cisco trained and authorized Networking Academy provider.

For information on the Cisco Networking Academy Program or to locate a Networking Academy, please visit www.cisco.com/edu.

Trademark Acknowledgments

All terms mentioned in this book that are known to be trademarks or service marks have been appropriately capitalized. Cisco Press or Cisco Systems, Inc., cannot attest to the accuracy of this information. Use of a term in this book should not be regarded as affecting the validity of any trademark or service mark.

Feedback Information

At Cisco Press, our goal is to create in-depth technical books of the highest quality and value. Each book is crafted with care and precision, undergoing rigorous development that involves the unique expertise of members of the professional technical community.

Readers' feedback is a natural continuation of this process. If you have any comments regarding how we could improve the quality of this book, or otherwise alter it to better suit your needs, you can contact us at networkingacademy@ciscopress.com. Please be sure to include the book title and ISBN in your message.

We greatly appreciate your assistance.

Publisher	John Wait
Editor-in-Chief	John Kane
Executive Editor	Carl Lindholm
Cisco Representative	Anthony Wolfenden
Cisco Press Program Manager	Sonia Torres Chavez
Cisco Marketing Communications Manager	Tom Geitner
Cisco Marketing Program Manager	Edie Quiroz
Production Manager	Patrick Kanouse
Development Editor	Karen Hicks
Project Editor	San Dee Phillips
Technical Editors	Jim Drennen, Arthur Toch, Arthur Tucker
Assistant Editor	Sarah Kimberly
Copy Editor	Cris Mattison

CISCO SYSTEMS

Corporate Headquarters
Cisco Systems, Inc.
170 West Tasman Drive
San Jose, CA 95134-1706
USA
http://www.cisco.com
Tel: 408 526-4000
      800 553-NETS (6387)
Fax: 408 526-4100

European Headquarters
Cisco Systems Europe
11 Rue Camille Desmoulins
92782 Issy-les-Moulineaux
Cedex 9
France
http://www-europe.cisco.com
Tel: 33 1 58 04 60 00
Fax: 33 1 58 04 61 00

Americas Headquarters
Cisco Systems, Inc.
170 West Tasman Drive
San Jose, CA 95134-1706
USA
http://www.cisco.com
Tel: 408 526-7660
Fax: 408 527-0883

Asia Pacific Headquarters
Cisco Systems Australia,
Pty., Ltd
Level 17, 99 Walker Street
North Sydney
NSW 2059 Australia
http://www.cisco.com
Tel: +61 2 8448 7100
Fax: +61 2 9957 4350

Cisco Systems has more than 200 offices in the following countries. Addresses, phone numbers, and fax numbers are listed on the Cisco Web site at www.cisco.com/go/offices

Argentina • Australia • Austria • Belgium • Brazil • Bulgaria • Canada • Chile • China • Colombia • Costa Rica • Croatia • Czech Republic • Denmark • Dubai, UAE • Finland • France • Germany • Greece • Hong Kong • Hungary • India • Indonesia • Ireland Israel • Italy • Japan • Korea • Luxembourg • Malaysia • Mexico • The Netherlands • New Zealand • Norway • Peru • Philippines Poland • Portugal • Puerto Rico • Romania • Russia • Saudi Arabia • Scotland • Singapore • Slovakia • Slovenia • South Africa • Spain Sweden • Switzerland • Taiwan • Thailand • Turkey • Ukraine • United Kingdom • United States • Venezuela • Vietnam • Zimbabwe

Copyright © 2000, Cisco Systems, Inc. All rights reserved. Access Registrar, AccessPath, Are You Ready, ATM Director, Browse with Me, CCDA, CCDE, CCDP, CCIE, CCNA, CCNP, CCSI, CD-PAC, CiscoLink, the Cisco NetWorks logo, the Cisco Powered Network logo, Cisco Systems Networking Academy, Fast Step, FireRunner, Follow Me Browsing, FormShare, GigaStack, IGX, Intelligence in the Optical Core, Internet Quotient, IP/VC, iQ Breakthrough, iQ Expertise, iQ FastTrack, iQuick Study, iQ Readiness Scorecard, The iQ Logo, Kernel Proxy, MGX, Natural Network Viewer, Network Registrar, the Networkers logo, Packet, PIX, Point and Click Internetworking, Policy Builder, RateMUX, ReyMaster, ReyView, ScriptShare, Secure Script, Shop with Me, SlideCast, SMARTnet, SVX, TrafficDirector, TransPath, VlanDirector, Voice LAN, Wavelength Router, Workgroup Director, and Workgroup Stack are trademarks of Cisco Systems, Inc.; Changing the Way We Work, Live, Play, and Learn, Empowering the Internet Generation, are service marks of Cisco Systems, Inc.; and Aironet, ASIST, BPX, Catalyst, Cisco, the Cisco Certified Internetwork Expert Logo, Cisco IOS, the Cisco IOS logo, Cisco Press, Cisco Systems, Cisco Systems Capital, the Cisco Systems logo, Collision Free, Enterprise/Solver, EtherChannel, EtherSwitch, FastHub, FastLink, FastPAD, IOS, IP/TV, IPX, LightStream, LightSwitch, MICA, NetRanger, Post-Routing, Pre-Routing, Registrar, StrataView Plus, Stratm, SwitchProbe, TeleRouter, are registered trademarks of Cisco Systems, Inc. or its affiliates in the U.S. and certain other countries.

All other brands, names, or trademarks mentioned in this document or Web site are the property of their respective owners. The use of the word partner does not imply a partnership relationship between Cisco and any other company. (0010R)

Table of Contents

Introduction

Cisco Networking Academy Program IT Essentials II: Network Operating Systems Lab Companion supplements the online course and the *IT Essentials II: Network Operating Systems Companion Guide*. It provides hands-on experience as well as review questions to support the material covered, or it can stand alone as a basic network operating system lab manual.

It is extremely beneficial to complete *IT Essentials I: PC Hardware and Software* before starting this course, although it is not required.

IT Essentials II: Network Operating Systems Lab Companion and its companion titles from Cisco Press prepare students for the Server+ Certification exam and, when studied in conjunction with the Fundamentals of UNIX course and its related titles, the Linux+ Certification exam.

The topics covered in the book include the fundamentals of the network operating system, specifically Windows and Linux. You will learn the steps to prepare and successfully install a network operating system, configure the components, and troubleshoot when problems occur. Working with the network operating system, you will create users, manage file systems, and perform advanced tasks such as backing up data and firewall maintenance. In addition, you will work with security issues to develop an acceptable-use policy and implement the rules to protect against outside and inside threats.

You will find that your studies are best complemented by a text that describes the theory and foundational concepts introduced in the hands-on lab exercises. To that end, Cisco Press offers *Cisco Networking Academy Program IT Essentials II: Network Operating Systems Companion Guide*, which provides comprehensive explanations of network operating system topics. In addition, *Cisco Networking Academy Program IT Essentials II: Network Operating Systems Engineering Journal and Workbook* provides review questions and exercises that allow you to apply your knowledge and practice what you have learned.

Who Should Read This Book

This book is intended for students who want to pursue a career in information technology or want working knowledge of how a computer works, how to administer Windows 2000 and Linux Red Hat Network Operating Systems, and how to troubleshoot hardware and software issues. Students who will be seeking their Server+ or Linux+ certifications will find this book particularly useful.

This Book's Organization

This book is divided into chapters corresponding to the chapters of the *IT Essentials II: Network Operating Systems Companion Guide*.

- **Chapter 1**—Worksheets include operating system basics, Windows basics, and UNIX and Linux Desktop basics.

- **Chapter 2**—Worksheets identify different network types, the OSI model, and protocols used over a network.

- **Chapter 3**—Worksheets focus on network topologies, physical media types, and all the network devices.

- **Chapter 4**—Worksheets include the TCP/IP networking model, an overview of IPv4 addressing, and subnetting.

- **Chapter 5**—Worksheets provide a review of the NOS network services, Windows 2000 Active Directory, and Novell's NDS. The lab configures Linux as a client of NIS.

- **Chapter 6**—Worksheets cover the characteristics of a NOS, insight to Windows 2000, and some background about Linux.

- **Chapter 7**—Worksheets cover the planning of the install with the hardware requirements in mind. Also reviewed are the components that make up a server and the boot processes of Linux and Windows 2000.

- **Chapter 8**—A lab-intensive chapter that provides the opportunity to explore the basics of Windows 2000 as a NOS, form configuring IP addresses, using the CLI, planning and managing user accounts, creating groups, assigning NTFS permissions, and configuring FTP and Telnet. Also, the worksheets provide a review of the install of Windows 2000.

- **Chapter 9**—Labs and worksheets cover the Linux OS, including the installation of Linux, configuring network settings and the X server, and post installation applications.

- **Chapter 10**—A lab-intensive chapter that contains several media activities. A broad range of items are covered in this Linux administration chapter, including logon procedures, GUI and CLI interfaces, shells and editors, adding groups and users, controlling daemons, and creating a Samba server. Media activities include configuring file system files and setting password and permissions.

- **Chapter 11**—Labs and worksheets discuss backup methods and hardware, mapping a drive on the network, identifying bottlenecks, installing and configuring resource usage, and installing and configuring SNMP.

- **Chapter 12**—Labs cover installing and maintaining hardware in a Linux environment, using the HCL, and updating the servers OS and hardware.

- **Chapter 13**—Labs and worksheets focus on troubleshooting as it relates to the operating system using TCP/IP utilities and Windows 2000 diagnostic tools, as well as being prepared for any problem, by using redundancy.

- **Chapter 14**—Labs and worksheets focus on security of the network. Worksheets include network security threats, implementing security, and anti-theft devices. The lab involves creating a security checklist for the network.

This Book's Features

- This book contains several elements that help you learn about the network operating system installed on the server:

- **Objectives and Scenarios**—Each lab in this manual provides an objective, or a goal of the lab. The equipment required is listed, and a scenario is provided that allows you to relate the exercise to real-world environments.

- **Reflection Questions**—To demonstrate an understanding of the concepts covered, a reflection question is provided at the end of the lab. In addition, there are questions designed to elicit particular points of understanding. These questions help verify your comprehension of the technology being implemented.

The conventions that present command syntax in this book are the same conventions used in the *Cisco IOS Command Reference*:

- **Bold** indicates commands and keywords that are entered literally as shown. In examples (not syntax), bold indicates user input (for example, a **show** command).

- *Italic* indicates arguments for which you supply values.

- Braces ({ }) indicate a required element.

- Square brackets ([ ]) indicate an optional element.

- Vertical bars (|) separate alternative, mutually exclusive elements.

- Braces and vertical bars within square brackets (such as [x {y | z}]) indicate a required choice within an optional element. You do not need to enter what is in the brackets, but if you do, you have some required choices in the braces.

CompTIA Authorized Quality Curriculum

The contents of this training material were created for the CompTIA Server+ Certification exam and CompTIA Linux+ Certification exam covering CompTIA certification exam objectives that were current as of December 2002.

How to Become CompTIA Certified

This training material can help you prepare for and pass a related CompTIA certification exam or exams. In order to achieve CompTIA certification, you must register for and pass a CompTIA certification exam or exams.

In order to become CompTIA certified, you must

1. Select a certification exam provider. For more information, please visit www.comptia.org/certification/general_information/test_locations.asp.

2. Register for and schedule a time to take the CompTIA certification exam(s) at a convenient location.

3. Read and sign the Candidate Agreement, which will be presented at the time of the exam(s). The text of the Candidate Agreement can be found at www.comptia.org/certification/general_information/candidate_agreement.asp.

4. Take and pass the CompTIA certification exam(s).

For more information about CompTIA's certifications, such as their industry acceptance, benefits, or program news, visit www.comptia.org/certification/default.asp.

CompTIA is a nonprofit information technology (IT) trade association. CompTIA's certifications are designed by subject matter experts from across the IT industry. Each CompTIA certification is vendor-neutral, covers multiple technologies, and requires demonstration of skills and knowledge widely sought after by the IT industry.

To contact CompTIA with any questions or comments:

Please call + 1 630 268 1818

questions@comptia.org

Worksheet 1.1.6: Operating System Basics

1. LANs were first created by installing _____ in the PCs and then connecting the adapters using _____ wire.

2. As network servers became more powerful, they began to take on the functions once handled by _____ and _____.

3. Whether designed for a stand-alone desktop computer or a multi-user network server, all operating system software includes the following components:
_____, _____, and _____.

4. The _____ is a relatively small piece of code that is loaded into memory when the computer boots.

5. The _____ is the component of the OS that the user interacts with. It acts as a bridge between the user and the kernel.

6. Some GUI software can consume more than one hundred times the storage space of CLI software. Because GUIs are more complicated than CLIs, GUI software requires significantly more _____ and _____.

7. When deployed as NOSs, UNIX and Linux are often configured without _____components.

8. Fill in the following chart:

Operating System	Supported File System(s)
Windows 3.x	
Windows 95, 98, ME	
Windows NT, 2000	
Windows XP	
IBM OS/2	
Linux	

Worksheet 1.2.8: Microsoft Windows Basics

1. What are some reasons to use the CLI-based MS-DOS operating system?

_____

_____

_____

2. What are some disadvantages to using MS-DOS?

_____

_____

_____

3. It was not until _____ was released in 1990 that Microsoft established its user interface as a major force in the industry.

4. _____ is an environment in which programs share memory addresses and exchange information.

5. A more efficient form of multitasking used by Windows 9x, Windows NT, and Windows 2000 is called _____.

6. _____ was the first Microsoft operating system to have networking components built in.

7. Windows 95 features, not available with previous versions of Windows include _____, _____, _____, and _____.

8. Windows ME is generally recognized as part of the 9x family. List the main features of ME:

    a._____

    b._____

    c._____

    d._____

    e._____

9. Windows NT software features improved _____, _____, _____, and _____.

10. Microsoft positioned Windows NT as an operating system for _____ and _____.

11. Windows XP and XP Professional offer many of the key features associated with a NOS. List these key features:

a. _____

b. _____

c. _____

d. _____

12. Fill in the following chart:

Command	Result
dir	
cd *directory name*	
time	
date	
copy	
diskcopy [*source*][*destination*]	
attrib	
find *text string*	
help	

Worksheet 1.3.5: UNIX and Linux on the Desktop

1. When UNIX first started to be marketed commercially in the 1980s, it was used to run
   _____, not _____.

2. What are some of the different distributions of Linux?

   a. _____

   b. _____

   c. _____

   d. _____

   e. _____

   f. _____

3. Which distributions of Linux are making efforts to develop Linux as a viable operating
   system for the desktop?

   a. _____

   b. _____

   c. _____

4. Some advantages of Linux as a desktop operating system and network client include the
   following:

   _____

   _____

5. UNIX and Linux both rely on the _____ to display the GUI.

6. The _____ is the software responsible for sizing, positioning, and
   rendering the graphical windows that programs run in.

7. Users type commands that are interpreted by the _____, which in turn relays
   the user's instructions to the operating system and other programs.

8. What are some of the tasks that can be done with the linuxconf tool?

   _____

   _____

   _____

   _____

Worksheet 2.2.5: Types of Networks

1. What characteristics define a LAN-based network as opposed to a WAN-based network?

   _____

   _____

   _____

2. What are the three basic types of network topologies and what are the characteristics of each of these three network topologies?

   a.

   _____

   _____

   b.

   _____

   _____

   c.

   _____

   _____

3. What purpose does a CSU/DSU provide in a WAN link?

   _____

   _____

   _____

4. Briefly describe a peer-to-peer network and give examples of where this type of network can be implemented?

   _____

   _____

5. Describe a client/server network and give some examples of the benefits of using a client/server approach.

   _____

   _____

   _____

   _____

Worksheet 2.3.2: The OSI Reference Model

1. This layer is responsible for providing reliable and unreliable data connections:

   _____

2. This layer specifies how addresses are assigned and how packets of data are forwarded from one network to another toward the destination: _____

3. This layer corresponds to the network hardware (cabling, media) and determines how binary data is translated into electrical, optical, or other types of physical signals that are transmitted between systems: _____

4. This layer provides the connection point for applications. It specifies the details of how an application makes requests and how the application on another machine responds:

   _____

5. This layer establishes the rules of the conversation between two applications. For example, will they take turns speaking, or can they send and receive at the same time:

   _____

6. This layer specifies how packets of data are organized into frames on a particular type of network and the rules for inserting frames on to the network media:

   _____

7. This layer specifies the arrangement, or syntax, of the data that the application expects. For example, .gif, .jpeg, .mpeg, or .avi file extensions:

   _____

8. List the steps of encapsulation as if a user is creating the data to be sent out over the network to another user, and explain what the corresponding OSI layer does to prepare the data to be sent over the network.

   a.

   _____

   _____

   b.

   _____

   _____

   c.

   _____

   _____

   d.

   _____

   _____

   e.

   _____

   _____

9. What layer of the OSI model does a router operate?

_____

10. What layer of the OSI model does a switch operate?

_____

Worksheet 2.4.4: Network Protocols

1. What are some of the TCP/IP protocols used at the application layer?

   a.

   _____

   _____

   b.

   _____

   _____

   c.

   _____

   _____

   d.

   _____

   _____

2. What are the two main protocols used at the transport layer within the TCP/IP suite of protocols?

   a.

   _____

   _____

   b.

   _____

   _____

3. What are the defining characteristics of the Transmission Control Protocol?

   _____

   _____

   _____

   _____

   _____

   _____

   _____

   _____

4. What are the defining characteristics of the User Datagram Protocol?

_____

_____

_____

_____

_____

_____

_____

_____

_____

5. What are some of the TCP/IP protocols that function at the network layer of the OSI model.

a.

_____

_____

b.

_____

_____

c.

_____

_____

d.

_____

_____

e.

_____

_____

6. What is the protocol that you use in a Novell network to enable clients to locate the services that they require, such as print or file services from servers.

a.

_____

_____

b.

_____

_____

Worksheet 3.2.7: Network Topologies

1. Describe the difference between a physical and logical topology?

_____

_____

_____

_____

2. Draw an example of a Bus topology:

3. Draw an example of a Star topology:

4. Draw an example of an extended Star topology:

5. The chapter lists some advantages of a Star topology. What are the advantages and disadvantages of a Star topology?

ADVANTAGES	DISADVANTAGES

6. Draw an example of a Ring topology:

7. The chapter lists some advantages of a Ring topology? What are the advantages and disadvantages of a Ring topology?

ADVANTAGES	DISADVANTAGES

8. The _____ topology combines more than one type of topology. When a bus line joins two hubs of different topologies, the configuration is called a star bus.

9. In what scenario or environment would you use a hybrid topology?

_____

_____

_____

_____

Worksheet 3.3.3: Twisted Pair Cabling

1. Twisted wire pairs limit signal degradation caused by
_____ and _____.

2. Category 5 and 5e have a maximum data transfer rate of _____ Mbps.

3. What are the two types of twisted pair cabling?

_____

4. How is the category of UTP cabling determined?

_____

_____

5. Category 3 cabling has a maximum data transfer rate of _____ Mbps.

6. What categories of cabling are most commonly used on Ethernet connections?

_____

7. There are _____ or _____ twisted pairs in a UTP cable.

8. UTP cabling relies solely on the _____ effect produced by the twisted pair wires.

9. Twisted pair is a type of cabling that is used for _____ and _____ connections.

10. What is the difference between Category 5 and Category 5e cabling?

_____

_____

11. What is the reason for twisting the wire pairs?

_____

_____

12. What do UTP and STP stand for?

_____

_____

13. In a shielded twisted pair cable, each individual pair of wires is wrapped in a _____, and the four pairs of wires are wrapped in a _____ to further shield the wires from noise.

14. UTP Category 3 cabling is used for what type of connection?

_____

15. Category 3 cabling has _____ pair of wires.

Worksheet 3.3.5: Physical Media Types

True or False

1. _____ An advantage of coaxial cable is that you can run the cable for much longer distances between nodes than twisted-pair cable.

2. _____ Ethernet cable is known to be more difficult to install than thicknet/coaxial cable.

3. _____ When installing cable in a ceiling that must conform to fire codes and be fire retardant, you should use PVC grade cable.

4. _____ Coaxial cable is the most common cable type that is used in Ethernet networks.

5. _____ STP reduces electrical noise, both within the cable (crosstalk) and from outside the cable (EMI and RFI).

6. _____ Fiber-optic cable provides faster bandwidth speeds than Ethernet cable and provides for greater signal integrity over long distances. It is also not susceptible to crosstalk and EMI because it uses beams of light to carry signals instead of copper wiring.

7. _____ FHSS and DSSS are two approaches currently being used to implement spread spectrum for wireless LAN transmissions.

8. _____ A benefit of wireless networks is that they are entirely secure on the signaling frequency and not easily monitored by people not on the network.

9. _____ The most popular type of cabling used in an Ethernet network is Category 3 UTP.

Worksheet 3.4.3: Network Devices

1. Define the following terms:

   a. Active hub

   _____

   b. Passive hub

   _____

   c. Intelligent hub

   _____

   d. Bridge

   _____

   e. Switch

   _____

   f. Router

   _____

2. Sometimes hubs are called _____ because they serve as a central connection point for an Ethernet LAN.

3. _____ can be computers with special network software installed on them or they can be other devices built by network equipment manufacturers.

4. Hubs operate at the _____ layer of the OSI model.

5. A _____ has many ports with many network segments connected to them. A _____ chooses the port to which the destination device or workstation is connected.

6. _____ are the most sophisticated internetworking devices discussed so far and operate at the network layer of the OSI model.

7. _____ operate at the data link layer of the OSI model.

Worksheet 4.1.2: The TCP/IP Network Model

1. Fill in the blank TCP/IP model as it corresponds to the OSI model:

OSI Model	TCP/IP Model
Application	
Presentation	
Session	
Transport	
Network	
Data Link	
Physical	

2. _____ and _____ are TCP/IP-based applications used for file transfer and are located at the application layer of the TCP/IP network model.

3. List some of the other protocols that function at the application layer.

   a.

   _____

   b.

   _____

   c.

   _____

   d.

   _____

   e.

   _____

4. Unlike the transport layer of the OSI model, which defines protocols such as Novell's SPX, the TCP/IP transport layer defines only _____ and _____.

5. _____ is achieved through the use of a technique called windowing, which allows communicating hosts to negotiate how much data is transmitted during a given period.

6. _____ help define and keep track of all the different types of conversations that are taking place throughout the network.

7. Fill in the blank spaces with the appropriate port number that corresponds to the protocol:

FTP	Telnet	SMTP	DNS	TFTP	SNMP	RIP

8. The system administrator has the ability to specify which types of traffic are allowed into a network by permitting or denying Internet traffic based on these port numbers. This process of filtering based on port numbers is usually accomplished with _____ or _____ devices.

9. The _____ layer of the TCP/IP model, also sometimes called the network layer, defines addressing and path selection.

10. The following are some of the protocols defined at this layer:

   a.
   _____

   b.
   _____

   c.
   _____

   d.
   _____

11. _____ finds the MAC address of a host, switch, or router, when given its IP address.

12. The _____ layer defines TCP/IP-specific functions that are related to the preparation of data for transmission over the physical media, including addressing. This layer also specifies what types of media can be used for the data transmission.

Worksheet 4.2.2: IPv4 Addressing Overview

1. Convert the binary number 1010 to decimal:

_____

2. Convert the binary number 11110000 to decimal:

_____

3. Convert the binary number 10101111 to decimal:

_____

4. Convert the decimal number 100 to binary:

_____

5. Convert the decimal number 249 to binary:

_____

6. Convert the decimal number 128 to binary:

_____

7. Convert the decimal number 65 to binary:

_____

8. Convert the decimal number 63 to binary:

_____

9. Convert the decimal number 198 to binary:

_____

10. Convert the decimal number 400 to binary:

_____

Worksheet 4.2.8: Subnetting

1. Define subnetting:

_____

_____

_____

_____

2. 210.58.101.5 is a Class _____ address.

3. 10.2.1.1 is a Class _____ address.

4. 163.58.101.5 is a Class _____ address.

5. Define the term subnet mask:

_____

_____

_____

_____

6. You are using a Class C subnet mask; how many hosts are you allowed to have on this subnet?

_____

7. You are using a Class A subnet mask; how many hosts are you allowed to have on this subnet?

_____

8. You are using 22 bits for subnetting your network. How many hosts are you allowed to have on this subnet and what is your subnet mask?

_____

9. You are using 20 bits for subnetting your network. How many hosts are you allowed to have on this subnet and what is your subnet mask?

_____

10. You are using 27 bits for subnetting your network. How many hosts are you allowed to have on this subnet and what is your subnet?

_____

Worksheet 5.1.1: Network/NOS Services

Match each term with its description:

1. _____ File Sharing   a. Telnet

2. _____ Remote Administration   b. SMTP, POP3, IMAP

3. _____ Network Administration   c. HTTP

4. _____ Internet Mail   d. NFS

5. _____ World Wide Web Server   e. DHCP

6. _____ Directory Services (Internet)   f. FTP, TFTP

7. _____ Automatic Network Address Configuration   g. DNS, LDAP

8. _____ File Transfer   h. SNMP

Worksheet 5.3.3: Windows 2000 Active Directory

1. The Active Directory information is stored in three files:

   a. _____

   b. _____

   c. _____

2. _____ is the means by which Windows 2000 administrators control user desktops, automatically deploy applications, and set user rights.

3. The logical structure of Active Directory is based on units called _____.

4. Windows NT uses a flat domain structure, and Windows 2000 arranges domains in hierarchical_____.

5. How can Administrative Authority be delegated in Windows 2000 as opposed to Windows NT?

   _____

   _____

   _____

6. True or False: _____ Windows 2000 Active Directory needs only one DNS server per domain to operate.

7. True or False: _____ It is recommended that you have one domain controller per domain.

8. Active Directory uses _____to copy directory information between the domain controllers in a domain.

9. Define these two terms:

   Assigned permissions

   _____

   _____

   _____

   Inherited permissions

   _____

   _____

   _____

Worksheet 5.3.4: Novell NDS

1. What version of Novell began using the NDS directory structure and what did the previous versions use before Novell implemented NDS?

   a. _____

   b. _____

2. NDS can have two basic types of objects: _____ and _____.

3. Give three examples of a leaf object in the NDS directory structure:

   a. _____

   b. _____

   c. _____

4. Describe the way that permissions are assigned in NDS as opposed to Active Directory.

   _____

   _____

   _____

5. Although generally associated with the NetWare NOS, NDS can run on a variety of platforms. Novell provides NDS for the following platforms:

   a. _____

   b. _____

   c. _____

   d. _____

   e. _____

   f. _____

6. NDS _____ is Novell's cross-platform solution for integrated enterprise computing with directory-enabled applications.

Lab 5.3.5: Configuring Linux as a NIS Client

Estimated Time: 30 minutes

Objective

- To configure a Linux Red Hat system as a NIS Server and Client

Equipment

The following equipment is required for this exercise:

- Computer with Linux Red Hat 7.x installed

Scenario

As the system administrator of a large company, you need to enable some employees' computer systems to share a common set of user accounts, user groups, TCP/IP hostnames, and other information. To centralize the administrative efforts involved, you decide to configure a Linux Red Hat system as a NIS server to manage the database. You must also configure the employees' computer systems as NIS clients.

Procedures

Step 1: Setting Up a Linux System as a NIS Client

To configure a Linux system as a NIS master server, you must first configure as you would a NIS client. Use the following steps to configure a Linux system as a NIS client.

1. Make sure that you are logged in as the root user.

2. To set up a NIS client, get the NIS domain name, NIS master server name, and the NIS slave server names. In a true running network, these might already be configured; however, for the purposes of this lab, just make these names up.

3. Because you don't have a NIS domain name, you need to define one first. To do so, type the following command at the shell prompt:

   ```
   domainname Ciscotest
   ```

4. This command sets the NIS domain name to Ciscotest. To verify that you set the NIS domain name properly, type the following command at the shell prompt:

   ```
   domainname
   ```

5. Typing this command sets only the NIS domain name temporarily, and when you reboot your system, this information is erased unless you configure your system to run this command every time your system boots up. You can use many methods to force a Linux system to run commands upon startup, many of which you have learned or will learn in this course. One easy method is to edit the /etc/init.d/network file.

First, type the following command at the shell prompt to view the /etc/init.d/network file, and so that you configure your system properly:

```
vi /etc/init.d/network
```

With this file open, press the **i** key on the keyboard to enter insert mode. Use the arrow keys to navigate to the ninth (9th) line and enter the following text:

```
# Set the NIS domain name.
domainname Ciscotest
```

Next, close this file by pressing the **Esc** key and type

:wq

Then, press the **Enter** key.

At this point, you should be back at the shell prompt.

6. Your next step is to set up the /etc/yp.conf file. The ypbind daemon needs to know what the NIS domain name is and what the name of your NIS servers are for it to work properly. The ypbind daemon is the process that runs the NIS service on the system. This information is contained in the /etc/yp.conf file; therefore, you need to edit this file with the proper information. To do so, you first need to open this file so that it can be edited. To do this, enter the following command at the shell prompt:

```
vi /etc/yp.conf
```

7. You should now have the vi editor open with the contents of the /etc/yp.conf file in view. Just as you did in the previous step, enter insert mode to make the proper configuration change. After you enter insert mode, navigate to the bottom of the text and enter the following lines of text:

```
domain Ciscotest server Phoenix1
```

This defines the name of the NIS master server. If the network consists of NIS slave servers, also enter them here. For example, you can add more lines directly under the text you just entered. Go ahead and do this now. Enter the following text in this file:

```
domain Ciscotest server Phoenix1
domain Ciscotest server Tempe1
domain Ciscotest server Scottsdale1
```

Next, close this file by pressing the **Esc** key, and type:

:wq

Then, press the **Enter** key.

At this point, you should be back at the shell prompt.

UXBRIDGE COLLEGE
LEARNING CENTRE

8. For you to run NIS as a client, start the ypbind and ypwhich daemons. The ypbind daemon performs two functions, the master and slave functions. The master process handles requests for information from the NIS server, and the slave process checks the bindings. The ypwhich daemon finds the NIS server. Starting these daemons and configuring them to run automatically every time the system is booted up is fairly simple. To do this, type the following command at the shell prompt:

```
/sbin/chkconfig ypbind on
```

There are other ways to accomplish this, but this might be the easiest way.

9. At this point, the Linux system should be set up to run as a NIS client. If this system was, in fact, connecting to an actual NIS server, you could use the ypwhich and ypcat hosts commands to test connectivity; however, if this is not the case, these commands return error messages.

Reflection

Configuring a Linux system can be useful. What are some circumstances in which using NIS is beneficial and some circumstances in which using NIS is not beneficial?

_____

_____

_____

_____

_____

_____

_____

_____

_____

_____

Worksheet 6.1.6: Characteristics of a Network Operating System

1. What is the function of an operating system?

_____

_____

_____

_____

2. Compare and contrast a PC operating system and a NOS:

_____

_____

_____

_____

3. Define the term multitasking system:

_____

_____

_____

_____

4. To achieve higher execution speeds, some systems are equipped with more than one processor. Such systems are called _____systems.

5. _____ means that the server systems must be able to function effectively under heavy load and be able to survive the failure of one or more processes or components without experiencing a general system failure.

6. What are the five criteria for choosing a NOS?

   a. _____

   b. _____

   c. _____

   d. _____

   e. _____

7. Describe the benefits that scalability adds to a NOS?

_____

_____

_____

_____

Worksheet 6.2.4: Windows NT/2000

1. A _____ is a grouping of computers and users that serves as a boundary of administrative authority.

2. Microsoft uses the term _____ to describe the logon authentication servers that hold a copy of the security accounts database.

3. NT runs DOS and older Windows programs in _____. Using this method, if one application crashes, it does not affect other applications or require a reboot of the operating system.

4. Windows NT provides an administrative tool called the _____ that is accessed from the domain controller, which creates, manages, and removes domain user accounts.

5. The _____ controls the authentication process when a user logs into the domain.

6. _____ technology allows an administrator to add components to the system, and the OS automatically recognizes and installs the drivers for the device.

7. Administrative tasks in Windows 2000 use a common framework, the

_____.

8. Compare and contrast the four operating systems in the Windows 2000 family of operating systems.

   a. Windows 2000 Professional:

   _____
   _____
   _____

   b. Windows 2000 Server:

   _____
   _____
   _____

   c. Windows 2000 Advanced Server:

   _____
   _____
   _____

   d. Windows .NET Server:

   _____
   _____
   _____

Worksheet 6.3.4: Linux

1. Linux is_____, which means that you'll find versions running on name brand or clone PCs, Apple Macintoshes, Sun workstations, or Digital Equipment Corporation Alpha-based computers.

2. The _____ provides a trademark for software developers who want to share their code with others, who are then free to modify and redistribute the code.

3. _____ operating systems are used on high-end workstations such as Silicon Graphics and Sun machines.

4. What are some of the most popular or well-known versions of Linux?

   a. _____

   b. _____

   c. _____

   d. _____

   e. _____

   f. _____

5. Recently, versions of Linux that fit on one or two floppy disks have been created. One such trimmed version is _____, which fits on one disk.

6. Windows clients can access Linux servers without client software if the Linux servers run _____, which is a program that uses the _____ application layer protocol.

7. What are the criteria for meeting the Open Source trademark?

   _____

   _____

   _____

   _____

   _____

   _____

   _____

   _____

   _____

Worksheet 7.1.3: Planning the Installation

1. Name five items that you need to verify prior to the actual installation:

_____

_____

_____

_____

_____

2. List two things that need to be checked at the installation site before bringing in the equipment: _____

3. What is a digital multimeter? _____

   What would a correct reading be if you were in Africa? _____

4. What does UPS stand for? _____

   How large should a UPS be for a server room? _____

5. What is the heat load of a server room measured in? _____

6. What is the ideal temperature in a server room? _____

7. What ensures proper airflow and adequate cooling in the server room?

_____

_____

8. Why is it a good idea to test the network connection before installing?

_____

_____

_____

Worksheet 7.1.4: Server Components

1. List three components of a typical server:

_____

_____

_____

True and False Questions

1. Multiple NICs can be installed on one server.

2. RAID controllers can be configured after the network operating system is installed.

3. SCSI-2 and SCSI-3 use the same cables to connect to a device.

4. A SCSI external cable and internal cable look different.

5. Only CD-R and CD-RW devices can be used for backups.

6. A UPS can monitor the server only by a serial or USB cable.

**Fill in the blank with the correct word. Each term can be used only once:
KVM, Disk Drives, DVD, Memory, Processors, Server Chassis, Server Rack, 3.5
floppy, CD-ROM**

1. Three devices, from the preceding list that are commonly found in desktop computer systems are also found in a server system. _____, _____, and _____.

2. _____ allows one keyboard/video/mouse to be hooked up to multiple network servers.

3. IDE and SCSI are two different types of _____.

4. Network servers require a large amount of _____.

5. _____ come in tower configuration or rack-mount configuration.

6. Network servers normally have more than one _____.

7. The _____ is a place to mount server components.

Worksheet 7.1.5: Hardware Requirements

Fill in the following charts with the correct information:

1. Windows 2000 Advanced Server:

Computer/Processor	
Memory	
Hard Disk	
Drive	
Display	
Peripheral	

2. Windows XP Professional:

Computer/Processor	
Memory	
Hard Disk	
Drive	
Display	
Peripheral	

3. Linux Red Hat 7.1:

Computer/Processor	
Memory	
Hard Disk	
Drive	
Display	
Peripheral	

Worksheet 7.1.8: File Systems

1. What are the file systems that Windows 2000 Server supports?

   1. _____ _____ _____ _____
   2. _____ _____ _____ _____
   3. _____ _____ _____ _____

2. Name the different types of FAT and what each one contributes to the file system.

   1. _____ _____ _____ _____
   2. _____ _____ _____ _____
   3. _____ _____ _____ _____

3. What are the benefits of NTFS version 5 over the different FAT file systems?

   _____

   _____

   _____

4. How does the UNIX file system differ from the Windows file system?

   _____.

5. What is the name of the UNIX/Linux top-level directory of the file system?

   _____

6. Which is the oldest Linux file system?_____

7. Linux supports which file systems? _____

Lab 7.2.6: Adding Swap File Space in a Linux System

Estimated Time: 20 minutes

Objective

To assess and add swap space in a Linux Red Hat operating system

Equipment

The following equipment is required for this exercise:

- Computer with Linux Red Hat 7.x installed

Scenario

You are the system administrator of a large company. You have noticed that one of the Linux Apache web servers that your company uses for its internal website has been running slow, and most of its resources have been used up. You have used up most of the IT budget for the year, so adding more RAM is out of the question. You decide to add more swap space to the server.

Procedures

Step 1: Assessing Swap usage

To determine how much swap space you need to add, first look at some files to check and see how much of the system's memory is being used and how much is left.

1. Using the **free** command in Linux allows you to check system memory. Type the following command at the shell prompt:

```
free -m -t
```

How much physical memory is available and how much of that is used?

Step 2: Adding a Swap file

1. To add swap space on your system, you must add a swap file. The first step is to create a file that is equal in size to the swap file that is going to be created. To do this, use the **dd** command. Enter the following command at the shell prompt:

```
dd if=/dev/zero of=swap.swp bs=1024 count=131072
```

2. Next, the swap.swp file that was created needs to be started so that the Linux system can use it to swap memory to disk. By using the **mkswap** command, you can enable Linux to use the new swap file, but it will not be active. Enter the following command at the shell prompt:

   `mkswap -f /root/swap.swp` or type `/sbin/mkswap -f /root/swap.swp`

3. To make this swap file active, you need to use the **swapon** command. To make this swap file inactive, simply use the **swapoff** command in place of the **swapon** command. Enter the following command at the shell prompt:

   `swapon /root/swap.swp` or type `/sbin/swapon /root/swap.swp`

The swap file that was just created will not be used the next time that the system is rebooted unless that entry is made in /etc/fstab.

Reflection

Adding swap space by using this method is definitely the quickest and easiest way. However, it does have some drawbacks. By creating this swap file on a partition that is already being used, the file can become fragmented as the partition gets used more and more. What are some other options that can be done instead of adding a swap file with this method?

Worksheet 7.3.5.1: The Boot Process

1. The Windows 2000 boot process occurs in five stages:

   a. _____

   b. _____

   c. _____

   d. _____

   e. _____

2. The boot process is slightly different on non-Intel based systems because NTLDR is not needed. On these systems, a file called _____ performs this function.

3. What function controls the boot process and why?

   _____

   _____

   _____

   _____

   _____

   _____

   _____

4. During the _____, a computer tests its memory and verifies that it has all the necessary hardware, such as a keyboard, mouse, and so on.

5. After the POST routine is complete, the computer locates a boot device and loads the _____ into memory, which in turn locates the active partition and loads it into memory. This component of the boot process allows the operating system to load into RAM.

6. What is the name of the Operating System Loader file, which begins loading the operating system?

   _____.

7. The _____ file is used only in the event that the computer is set up to dual boot.

8. If the computer is not dual booting, NTLDR runs_____, which gathers information about the computer hardware.

9. Four additional steps take place at the point in the boot process that the graphical user interface (GUI) is first seen, and a status bar shows that the GUI is now loading. What are these four steps and briefly describe what occurs in each step?

a. _____

_____

_____

_____

b. _____

_____

_____

_____

c. _____

_____

_____

_____

d. _____

_____

_____

_____

Worksheet 7.3.5.2: Linux Boot Process

True or False

1. _____ The Linux boot process is much more complicated and involved than the Windows 2000 boot process.

2. _____ The NTLDR file in Windows performs the same function as the LILO file in Linux.

3. _____ The boot processes of Windows compared to Linux are different.

4. _____ The Linux kernel file works in a similar fashion to only the NTOSKRNL file in Windows.

5. _____ What file in Linux performs a function similar to the SMSS.exe file in Windows?

Lab 8.1.1: Installation Demonstration of Windows 2000

Estimated Time: 50 Minutes

Objective

In this lab, you learn how to install and run through a Windows 2000 installation step by step.

Equipment

The following equipment is required for this exercise:

- Computer with no operating system installed or a computer with at least one blank partition with no operating system on it

- Processor of Pentium class or better

- Minimum of a 2-GB hard drive with at least 1 GB of free space

Scenario

A new computer has been delivered and you are assigned the task of installing Windows 2000 Professional.

Procedures

In this lab, you learn how to install the Windows 2000 Professional operating system.

Installing Windows 2000 Professional

Note: In this lab, Windows 2000 Professional will be installed from the CD.

1. Turn on the computer and enter **CMOS setup.** (During the boot process, the screen indicates the keystroke to enter CMOS setup.) When you hear the beep, press the appropriate keys to enter CMOS setup.

2. Using the arrow keys, select the **BIOS FEATURES SETUP** and press the **Enter** key.

3. If the boot sequence is not set to boot from the CD-ROM first, scroll down and change the boot sequence to boot from the CD-ROM first by using the Page Up, Page Down, + or - keys.

4. Insert the Windows 2000 CD into the CD-ROM drive.

5. Press the **Escape** key once.

6. Select **Save**, exit setup, and press the **Enter** key.

7. Type **Y** and press the **Enter** key.

8. If prompted to press any key to boot from the CD-ROM, press any key. You should receive the message "Setup is configuring your computer's hardware configuration …".

9. A blue screen appears with the message "Windows 2000 Setup" (see Figure 8-1). Be patient while Windows 2000 loads files.

Figure 8-1   Windows 2000 Setup Screen

10. The next screen offers you three options (see Figure 8-2). This lab uses option 1. Press **Enter** to begin installation of Windows 2000.

Figure 8-2   Windows 2000 Install Options Screen

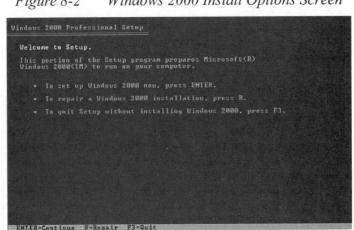

11. Press **F8** to accept the Licensing Agreement (see Figure 8-3).

Figure 8-3   End-User License Agreement

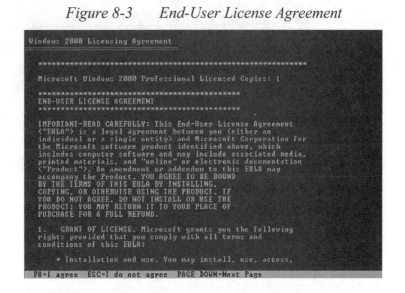

12. Windows now shows all partitions (see Figure 8-4), and asks you to select which one to install to. If no partitions are available, select unpartitioned space to create a partition and install Windows on this partition. If a partition already exists, follow the options on the screen to delete it. Press the **Enter** key to begin the installation.

Figure 8-4   Partitioning Screen

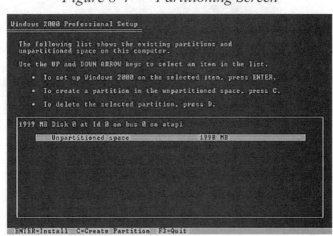

13. From the screen in Figure 8-5, select **Format the partition using the NTFS file system** and press **Enter**. NTFS offers more security than FAT32 and should be the file system of choice when installing Windows 2000.

Figure 8-5   Formatting Options Page

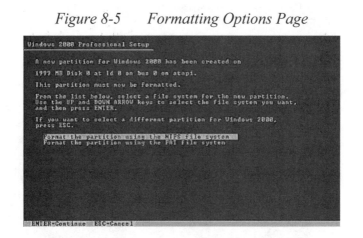

14. Windows formats the partition with the specified file system. This can take several minutes, depending on the size of your hard drive (see Figure 8-6).

Figure 8-6   Formatting Progress Indicator Page

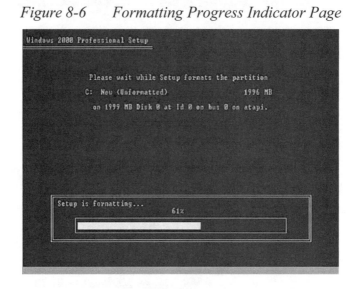

15. Setup now checks your disk and copies files needed to install Windows 2000 (see Figure 8-7).

Figure 8-7   Copying Files Progress Indicator Page

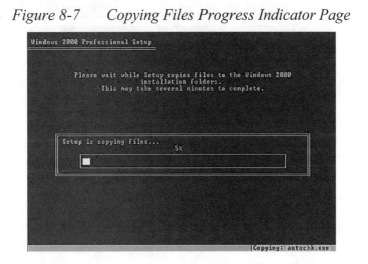

16. The system reboots and continues with setup. Do not press a key to boot from the CD-ROM.

17. Click **NEXT** when the Setup Wizard in Figure 8-8 appears, and setup starts detecting and installing devices on your computer. If you do not, Windows automatically goes to the next step.

Figure 8-8   GUI Setup Wizard Screen

18.   Click **Next** when the Regional Settings window in Figure 8-9 appears.

Figure 8-9   Regional Settings Screen

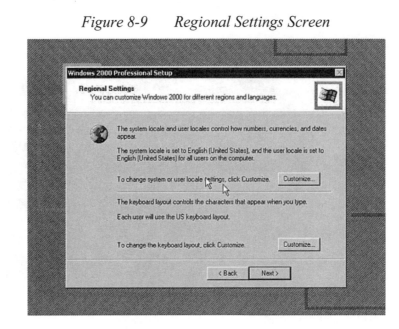

19 In the screen in Figure 8-10, enter **Administrator** for the name and **CWA** for the organization.

20. Click **Next**.

Figure 8-10   Personalize the Operating System Screen

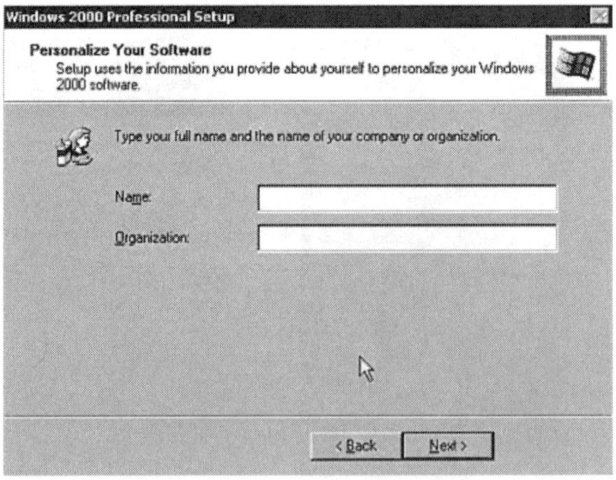

49

21. In the screen in Figure 8-11, enter the product key that came with the Windows 2000 CD.

Figure 8-11   Windows 2000 Product Key

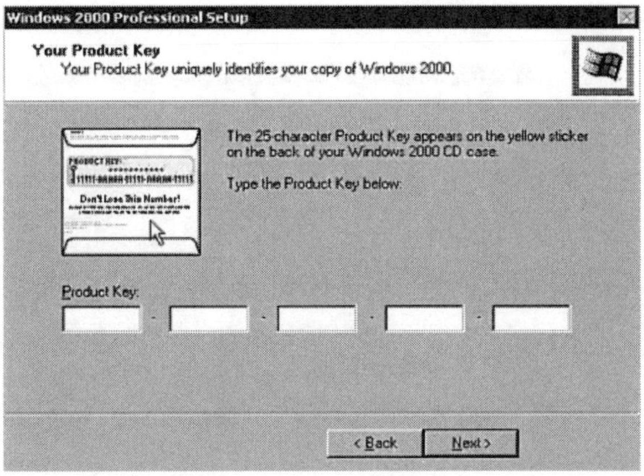

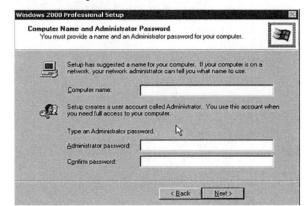

22. Click **Next**.

23. In the screen in Figure 8-12, enter **KIT2** for the Computer name text box and **password** in the Administrator password and the Confirm password text boxes. Be sure to enter the password in lowercase letters because Windows 2000 is case-sensitive.

Figure 8-12   Computer Name and Admin Password Settings

24. Click **Next**.

25. In the screen in Figure 8-13, enter the correct date, time, and regional area for your location.

Figure 8-13 Date and Time Settings

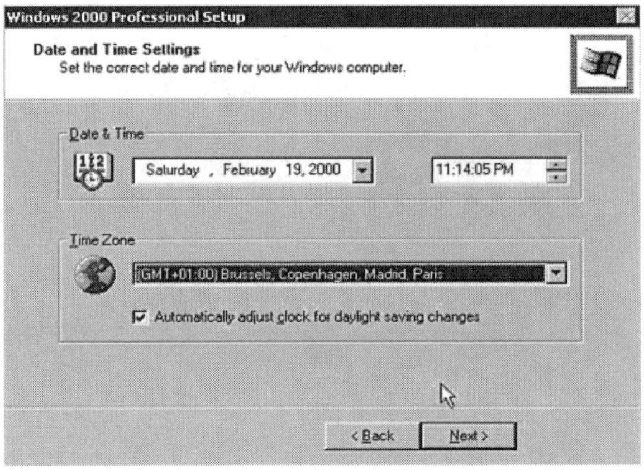

26. Click **Next**.

27. In the screen in Figure 8-14, click **Next** to do a typical installation.

Figure 8-14 Network Settings Screen

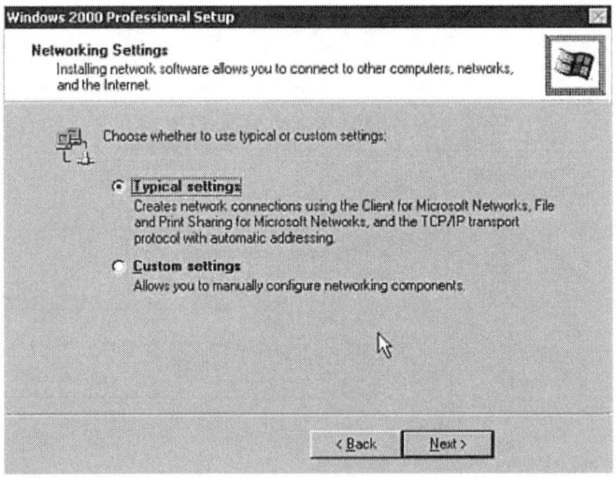

28. In the screen in Figure 8-15, select **Yes, make this computer a member of the following domain:** and click **Next** to install this computer as a member of the workgroup named WORKGROUP. This takes several minutes.

Figure 8-15   Workgroup or Domain Assignment Screen

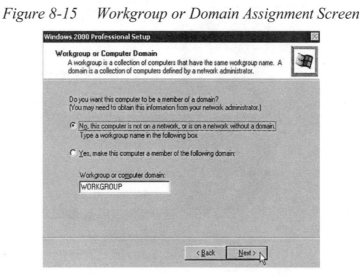

29. Remove the Windows 2000 CD and click **Finish** in the screen in Figure 8-16 to restart Windows.

Figure 8-16   Completing Setup Screen

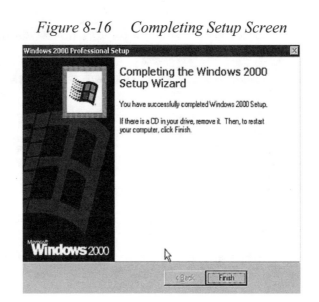

30. Click **Next** when the Welcome to the Network Connection Wizard window in Figure 8-17 appears.

Figure 8-17   Network Connection Configuration

31. In the screen in Figure 8-18, select the radio button **Users must enter a user name and password to use this computer**.

32. Click **Next**.

Figure 8-18   Network Identification Configuration

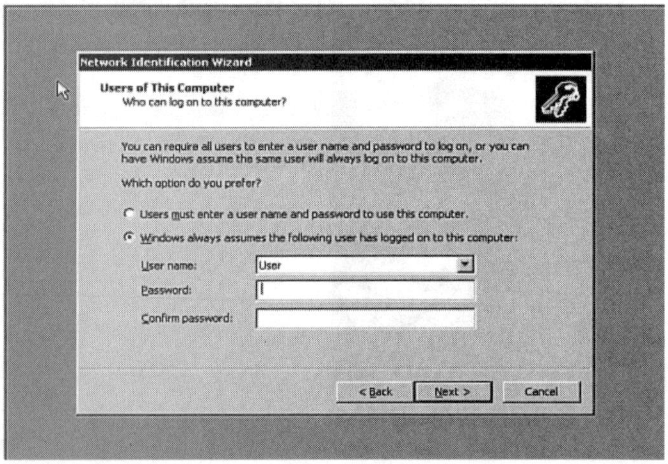

33. Click **Finish** to complete the Network Identification Wizard (see Figure 8-19).

Figure 8-19   Network Identification: Final Tasks

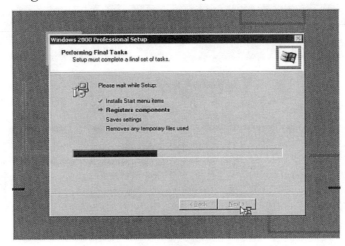

34. The logon box appears. Log on with the Administrator account and password that you created during setup.

35. Enter the password in the password text box and click **OK**.

36. The system now logs you on and launches the Windows 2000 Desktop.

37. Remove the check from the **Show this screen at startup** radio button in Figure 8-20.

Figure 8-20   Network Identification Configuration

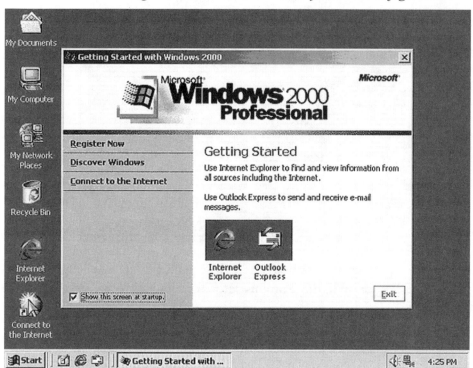

38. Click **Exit**.

Windows 2000 has now successfully installed.

Troubleshooting

Before proceeding with the installation, confirm that you have the proper hardware requirements in your system. Also make sure that you are installing the operating system on a blank partition or a hard drive that has enough space to install the operating system.

When the installation is complete, check hardware settings to see if the network card driver is installed. Upgrade the driver if necessary.

Ping your instructor's server to check network connectivity.

Worksheet 8.1.1: Installing the OS

1. Microsoft has a tool called the _____ that you can use before installing Windows 2000 to verify that the hardware actually works with Windows 2000.

2. The four steps in the Windows 2000 installation process are as follows:

   a. _____

   b. _____

   c. _____

   d. _____

3. True or False: _____ You can convert a drive from FAT to NTFS and from NTFS to FAT.

4. By default, the Windows 2000 operating system files are installed in the _____ folder.

5. During the installation, a built-in Administrator account is created that has privileges to make any changes to the computer. The password for this account can be changed later but only by the user that has _____ to the system.

6. During the Networking Component stage of the installation, three key components install. What are they and what do they do?

   a. _____

   b. _____

   c. _____

7. What are the four types of installations that can be performed when installing Windows 2000?

   a. _____

   b. _____

   c. _____

   d. _____

8. If you want to view Microsoft's HCL, how would you accomplish this without going to Microsoft's website?

   _____

   _____

   _____

Lab 8.1.2: Configuring an IP Address and Default Gateway in Windows 2000

Estimated Time: 20 Minutes

Objective

In this exercise, you configure a Windows 2000 Professional IP address.

Equipment

The following equipment is required for this exercise:

- Computer system running Windows 2000 Professional
- Network connection from the system to a hub, switch, or some other host
-

Scenario

The Air Guitar Company has installed a server running Windows 2000. The company asked you to configure the system with an IP address and subnet mask.

Procedures

Before beginning this lab, make sure the Windows 2000 system is ready for you to log in. Power the computer on, if necessary.

Ask your instructor or a lab technician for the appropriate IP address information for your system. Record that information in the table provided:

Host IP Address Configuration	
IP address:	
Subnet mask:	
Default gateway:	
DNS Server:	
DHCP Server:	Enabled/Disabled

Note: If your instructor provides a Dynamic Host Configuration Protocol (DHCP) server, write the IP range down and the subnet mask and default gateway for your network.

Step 1

Log in as Administrator. On a typical system, only the administrator can configure an IP address.

Step 2: Configuring TCP/IP to Use a Static IP Address

Right-click **My Network Places** and then click **Properties**. This displays the Network and Dial-Up Connections window.

1. Right-click **Local Area Connection** and then select **Properties**.

2. The Local Area Connection properties dialog box appears.

3. Click **TCP/IP**, verify that the check box to the left of the entry is selected, and then click **Properties**.

4. The Internet Protocol (TCP/IP) Properties dialog box appears.

5. Click **Use The Following IP Address**.

6. In the IP Address box, Subnet Mask box, and Default Gateway box, type the values that you entered in the table in the Procedures step of this lab.

7. Click **OK**. You return to the Local Area Connection properties dialog box.

8. Click **OK** to close the Local Area Connection properties dialog box.

9. Minimize the Network And Dial-Up Connections window.

Step 3: Testing the Static TCP/IP Configuration

1. Open the command prompt. Select **Start** > **Run** and type **cmd.exe** in the window to display a command prompt.

2. At the command prompt, type **ipconfig /all** and press **Enter**.

This displays the TCP/IP information configured on the physical and logical adapters in your computer.

3. Record the current TCP/IP configuration settings for your local area connection in the following table.

Current IP Address Configuration	
IP address:	
Subnet mask:	
Default gateway:	
DNS Server:	
DHCP Server:	Enabled/Disabled

Step 4: Testing the Configuration, with ICMP (Internet Control Messaging Protocol), Better Known as Ping

1. At the command prompt, type **ping xxx.xxx.xxx.xxx** (replace the **xxx.xxx.xxx.xxx** with the IP address that you entered for your computer, for example, ping 10.1.1.5).

This sends messages to your system to test if the IP address information was entered correctly.

If you get a successful reply such as the output in Figure 8-21, you have correctly configured your IP address.

Figure 8-21   Output of the Ping Command

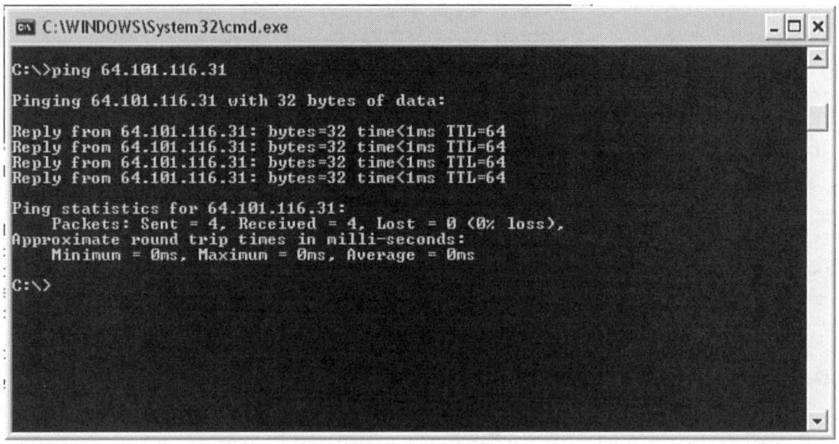

Troubleshooting

As an IT professional, configuring and troubleshooting TCP/IP can be a daily activity. Always double-check a static IP configuration. Most operating systems warn you when they detect another node on the network with the same IP address. Be careful when manually entering IP configuration settings, especially numeric addresses. The most frequent cause of TCP/IP connection problems is incorrectly entered IP address information.

Lab 8.2.1: Logging On to Windows 2000

Estimated Time: 10 Minutes

Objective

In this lab, you log on to Windows 2000.

Equipment

The following equipment is required for this exercise:

- Computer running Windows 2000 Professional

Background

The option to **Log on to Windows 2000 Professional** must be enabled to give users the ability to log on to either a network domain or a local computer.

The logon process is the main component of security for the Windows 2000 operating system. It defines who is accessing the computer and its network resources. It also specifies the rights and permissions the user has for accessing these resources.

Procedures

In this lab, you log on to the local computer by using the local administrator password. Logging on to the local computer as Administrator gives you full administrative control of this computer, but you will not have access to any network resources. You need to log on to the domain using a domain user account to have access to network resources.

Step 1: Logging On to the Local Computer

1. When you first start up your computer, the Windows 2000 logon screen in Figure 8-22 displays.

Figure 8-22   Windows 2000 Logon Screen

2. Log on with the following information:

> Username: **Administrator**
>
> Password: **cisco**

Passwords are case-sensitive and display only asterisks when they are entered.

3. Press the **Enter** key, or click the **OK** button to log on to the local Windows 2000 machine.

Step 2: Logging Off of Windows 2000

1. Before you can log on to Windows 2000 again as a new user, you must first log off the system. Click the **Start** button and select **Shut Down** to display the Shut Down Windows dialog box.

2. Select **Log off Administrator** from the drop-down box. The administrator is now be logged off and the system returns to the start-up screen.

Lab 8.2.2: Using the Windows 2000 GUI

Estimated Time: 15 Minutes

Objective

In this lab, you explore the basic features of the Windows GUI.

Equipment

The following equipment is required for this exercise:

- Computer system running Windows 2000 Professional with administrative tools enabled

Scenario

The Air Guitar Company installed a system running Windows 2000 Professional. The company asked you to log in with the Administrator account. Your task is to explore the basic features of the Windows GUI.

Procedures

Before beginning this lab, make sure that the Windows 2000 Professional system is powered on and ready for you to log in.

Step 1

After the computer boots, the Log On to Windows dialog box appears. Log in with the following information:

> Username: **Administrator**
>
> Password: **cisco**

When you finish entering the password, click the **Enter** button. If you typed the username and password correctly, the system authenticates you and gives you access to the computer.

Step 2

After user information is authenticated, the desktop environment in Figure 8-23 appears.

Figure 8-23   Windows 2000 Desktop

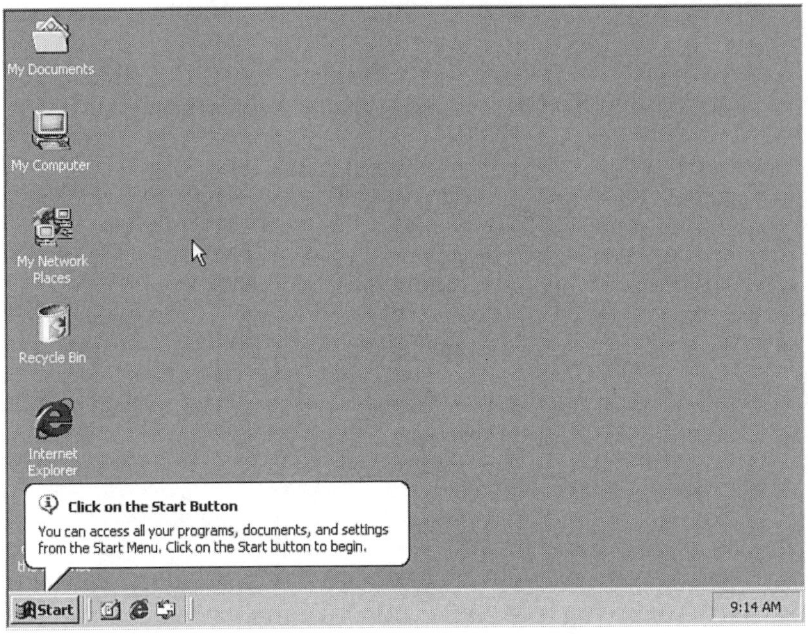

The desktop environment includes several icons and the taskbar. By default, the taskbar resides at the bottom of the screen. Windows is designed for a two-button mouse. The following table describes 5The function of left and right mouse buttons:

Mouse Button	Function
Left	Use to select and drag items.
Right	Use to bring up a menu for the selected object (when applicable).

You run applications by opening windows on the desktop. Windows include borders that can be dragged to resize the window and graphical buttons that can be clicked to minimize, maximize, restore, and close the window. The following table shows the window buttons and their function:

Window Button	Function
	Minimizes a window. Clicking its title on the taskbar can restore a minimized window. (The taskbar is part of the panel).
	Maximizes a window.
	Restores a maximized window to its original size.
	Closes a window. If the window contains an application running in the foreground, this option will terminate the application.

The Windows taskbar contains icons that start key applications or open menus. It also contains an area that displays the names of open windows. You can switch between these windows by clicking the names in the taskbar.

The following icons typically appear on the taskbar:

Taskbar Icon	Function
	Opens the Start Menu.
	Launches the Internet Explorer Web Browser (iexplore.exe). (This is a Quick Launch icon, and might not appear on all taskbars.)
	Minimizes all open windows to reveal the desktop. (This is a Quick Launch icon, and might not appear on all taskbars.)

The Windows Start Menu is typically the first place an administrator goes to perform a task.

Right-click the taskbar. Select **Properties** and click the **Advanced** tab. Check the box for Display Administrative Tools and click **OK**.

Click the **Start** button and select **Programs** from the menu. After the Programs submenu appears, select the **Administrative Tools** option, as shown in Figure 8-24:

Figure 8-24   Computer Management Toolbar

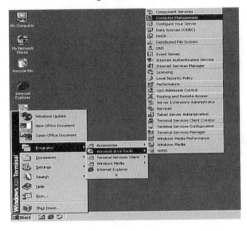

After you are in the Administrative Tools submenu, left-click **Computer Management**.

The Computer Management window offers centralized management that allows you to configure virtually all the system's key components, including the following (see Figure 8-25):

- Network services (such as mail, Web, DNS, SNMP)

- Shared folder

- Hardware devices (through Device Manager)

- Local users and groups

- Storage

Figure 8-25   Computer Management Toolbar

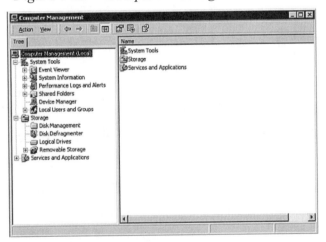

Windows 2000 system administrators typically use the Computer Management window to complete a majority of their administration tasks. You return to this window in future labs.

You explore some of the computer management features in the next step.

Step 3

The Event Viewer can track down most problems with your computer. Now that you are in the Computer Management window, click the plus sign (+) to the left of Event Viewer. The Management Tree expands to display all the logs kept by the Event Viewer.

The Event Viewer tracks, or logs, events on the system. If the system crashes or the administrator suspects a security problem, the Event Viewer can give some idea as to what happened.

1. What are the names of the logs shown in the expanded tree?

_____

Click the minus sign (-) next to Event Viewer to collapse the tree.

Next, click the plus sign (+) to the left of System Information and highlight **System Summary**, as shown in Figure 8-26.

Figure 8-26   System Summary

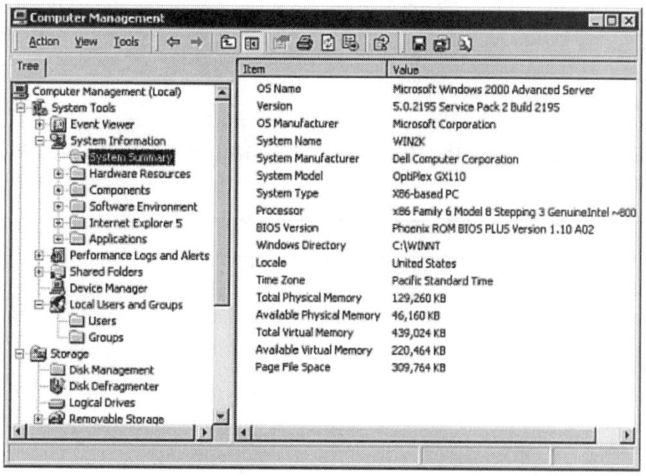

2. According to the output of the System Summary on your computer, what is the version number of the NOS? _____

3. Who is the system manufacturer?

_____

4. What type of processor does your computer have?

_____

5. What is the BIOS version of your system?

_____

6. What is the total amount of physical memory on the system?

_____

After you answer the previous questions, close the Computer Management window by clicking the **X** at the top right corner of the window.

Step 4

From the Start Menu, log off the system.

Reflection

Who should have access to the Computer Management window?

_____

_____

Lab 8.2.3: Using the Windows 2000 CLI

Estimated Time: 10 Minutes

Objective

In this lab, you learn how to use the Windows 2000 Command-Line Interface (CLI) by running and executing a few commands.

Equipment

The following equipment is required for this exercise:

- Computer with Windows 2000 Professional installed

Scenario

You are the system administrator for the XYZ Company and it is your job to administer the company's computers that have Windows 2000 Professional. You are going to be setting up a Telnet administration that is run from the command line and you need to become familiar with the process of working with the CLI.

Procedures

In this lab, you access the CLI. You learn and execute various helpful commands to become familiar with using the CLI and how it works.

Step 1: Opening the CLI

There are two ways to access the CLI:

1. Log on as the Administrator. On the taskbar, click **Start** > **Programs** > **Accessories**, and click the menu choice for Command Prompt.

2. On the taskbar, click **Start** > **Run**, and in the Open box type **cmd.exe**.

3. When the command prompt in Figure 8-27 opens, type **exit** to close the CLI.

Figure 8-27   Command-Line Interface

Step 2: Executing Commands and Navigating with the CLI

1. Press the **ALT + Enter** on the keyboard; the display switches to fill the entire screen with the Windows 2000 CLI.

2. Type **dir** at the C:\> prompt. This shows the contents of the C: drive.

3. Type **cd winnt** at the C:\> prompt and then dir. This shows the contents of the C:\Winnt folder.

4. Type **cd**. This brings you back to the C:\> prompt.

5. Type **edit autoexec.bat**. You can edit the autoexec.bat file with this command.

6. Press the **Alt + F7** key; or press **Alt** + the letter **F** to display the drop-down menu and go to exit and press **Enter** to get back to the command prompt.

7 .Type **ipconfig /all** to display the network configurations of your computer.

What is the IP address? _____

What is the DNS server address and the host name of the computer?

_____

Troubleshooting

Using the CLI can help you with troubleshooting a variety of problems when the GUI is not available. Using the CLI enables you to effectively access the operating system and make repairs without crashing the system.

Lab 8.2.4: Navigating the Windows 2000 File System with Windows Explorer and My Computer

Estimated Time: 15 Minutes

Objective

In this lab, you learn how to navigate the Windows 2000 file system with Windows Explorer. You also learn how to use the navigation tools provided by Windows 2000 to locate files and folders.

Equipment

The following equipment is required for this exercise:

- Computer running Windows 2000 Professional

- Marketing Folder with an Excel file named Spreadsheet.xls saved in the Marketing folder

Scenario

You are responding to a trouble call for a user at the XYZ Company. This user is unsure of how to locate a lost file. You need to show them various ways to navigate through the system to locate files.

Procedures

You use the Windows 2000 Explorer and My Computer to navigate files.

Step 1: Navigating the Windows 2000 File System Using Windows Explorer

1. Right-click the **My Computer** icon on the desktop or right-click the **Start** button and select **Explore** from the menu to get the screen in Figure 8-28.

Figure 8-28   My Computer

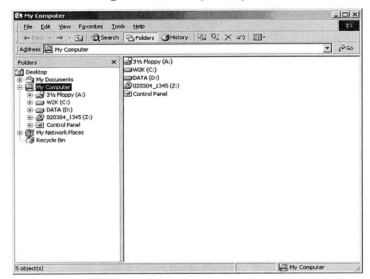

2. Locate the local Disk C:\ icon and click the plus sign (+) to expand the contents of the drive.

3. If you click directly on the drive, the contents of the drive appear on the right side of the screen.

4. On the left side menu of Windows Explorer, locate the Documents and Settings folder and click the plus sign (+) next to this folder. This displays the contents of the folder.

5. Click directly on the folder itself, and the contents of the Documents and Settings folder appear on the right side of the screen.

6. You have successfully navigated to the Administrative and All User folder using Windows Explorer.

7. Close the Windows Explorer window.

Step 2: Navigating the Windows 2000 File System Using My Computer

Double-click the **My Computer** icon located on the desktop.

1. This displays all the drives located on your system.

2. Click the folder view ⊞▾ button located on the menu bar. A drop-down menu displays the folder and file options in My Computer. Select the **Details** options to change this view. The Details view provides important information including the date last modified, size, and type.

3. Double-click the **Local Disk (C:)** icon to display the contents of the C:\ drive. Change the view to Details again, if necessary, to see the file information.

4. Locate the **Documents and Settings** folder and double-click it.

5. This displays the contents of the Documents and Settings folder. Within this folder, locate the Administrative and All User folder.

Reflection

There are various ways to navigate and to locate files and folders.

1. What is another way to locate files or folders, or to navigate the Windows 2000 file system?

_____

Lab 8.3.1: Adding Users in Windows 2000

Estimated Time: 10 Minutes

Objectives

In this lab, you describe the role and purpose of user accounts, and plan and create local and domain user accounts.

Equipment

The following equipment is required for this exercise:

- System running Windows 2000 with administrative tools enabled

Scenario

The Air Guitar Company installed a new system running Windows 2000. The company asked you to log on to the computer and create local accounts for two users.

Procedures

Before proceeding with this lab, you need to obtain from your instructor information to create two new users. You will need the following:

- usernames
- full names
- descriptions
- passwords

Additionally, you need the username, password, and domain to log on as the Administrator.

In this lab, you create two user accounts in Windows 2000. Log on as the Administrator and create the first user. While logged on as the first user, use the **Run As** command to gain Administrator privileges to create the second user.

Step 1

1. Log on as Administrator.

2. Go to: **Start** > **Programs** > **Administrative Tools** > **Computer Management** (see Figure 8-29).

Figure 8-29   Computer Management

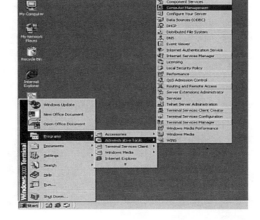

3. System Tools opens. Expand **Local Users and Groups** and. highlight **Users**.

4. Right-click the **Users** folder and select **New User,** as shown in Figure 8-30.

Figure 8-30   Adding a New User Account

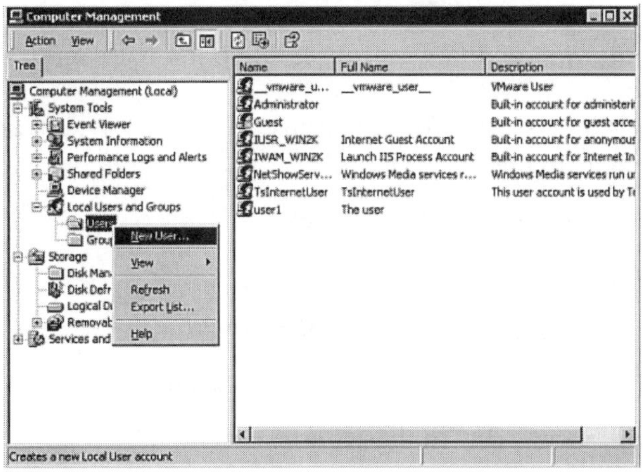

5. Create the first new user. Enter all information as provided by your instructor in the screen in Figure 8-31.

> *Note*: Make sure that all options are deselected.

Figure 8-31   New User Account Settings

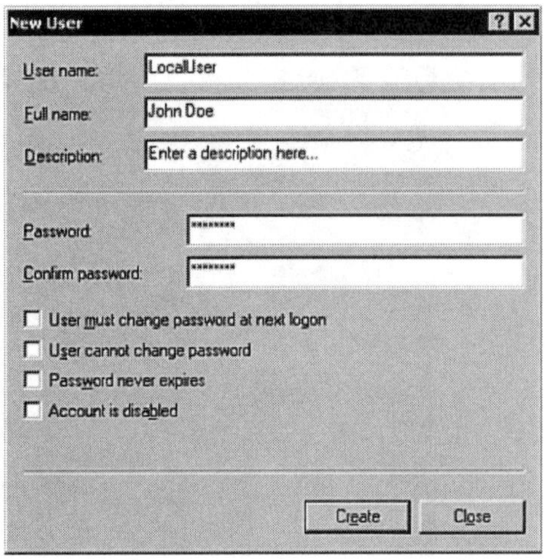

6. When finished, click the **Create** button.

   The new user has now been created.

7. Log off the system.

8. Using the account information that was just created, log back on to the system.

   Note: Because you are a new user, Administrative tools is not be available. Follow these steps to add Administrative tools to the Start Menu:

   a. Right-click the task bar and click **Properties**.

   b. Select the **Advanced** tab.

   c. Under the Start Menu settings, check the **Display Administrative Tools**.

   d. Click **Apply** and click **OK** to exit back to the desktop.

9. The second user will be added with the **Run as** command.

10. Go to: **Start** > **Programs** > **Administrative Tools** > **Computer Management**.

11. Right-click **Computer Management** and select **Run the program as the following user** (see Figure 8-32). Enter the Administrator account information and click **OK**.

Figure 8-32   Run as Administrator

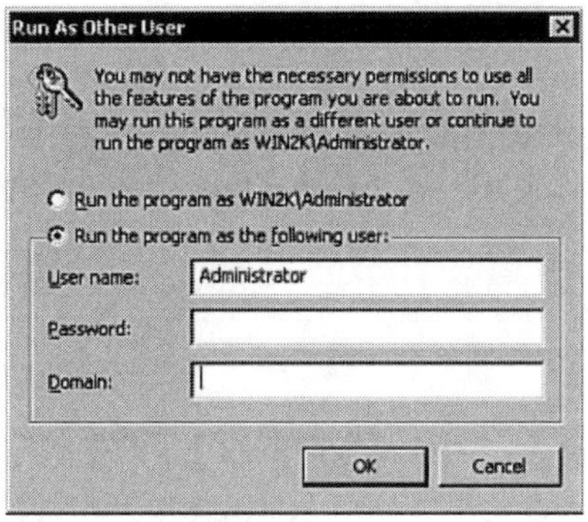

This grants administrator privileges to this instance of Computer Management only.

12. Repeat Steps 2 through 7 to create the second user.

Troubleshooting

To create accounts in Windows 2000, you must be either logged onto the computer as Administrator or operating the tools as Administrator with the Run as option. If you encounter problems while creating these accounts, verify that you have the necessary administrative privileges by logging off of the computer and logging on again using the Administrator account.

Reflection

1. What are some of the other applications found under the Administrative Tools of the Start Menu?

_____

_____

2. Is the Run as option available for any other Administrative Tools in Windows 2000?

_____

_____

3. Why is it important that only an administrator is allowed to create user accounts?

_____

_____

Lab 8.3.2: Managing User Accounts in Windows 2000

Estimated Time: 15 Minutes

Objective

In this lab, you learn how to manage user accounts using the Windows 2000 Professional operating system. Also discussed are the features and tools that manage user accounts.

Procedure

In this lab, you learn some of the Windows 2000 Professional techniques that manage user accounts after they are created. You use the studentA1 and the studentA2 accounts that you created in a previous lab.

Step 1: Changing User Account Properties

1. Log on to the system with the Administrator account.

2. Open the Computer Management screen by selecting **Administrative Tools** from the Start Menu.

3. Click the plus sign (+) sign next to the Local Users and Groups icon to expand it.

4 .Click the **Users** folder to display the list of users in the right side of the screen (similar to what you would see in Figure 8-33).

Figure 8-33   Local User

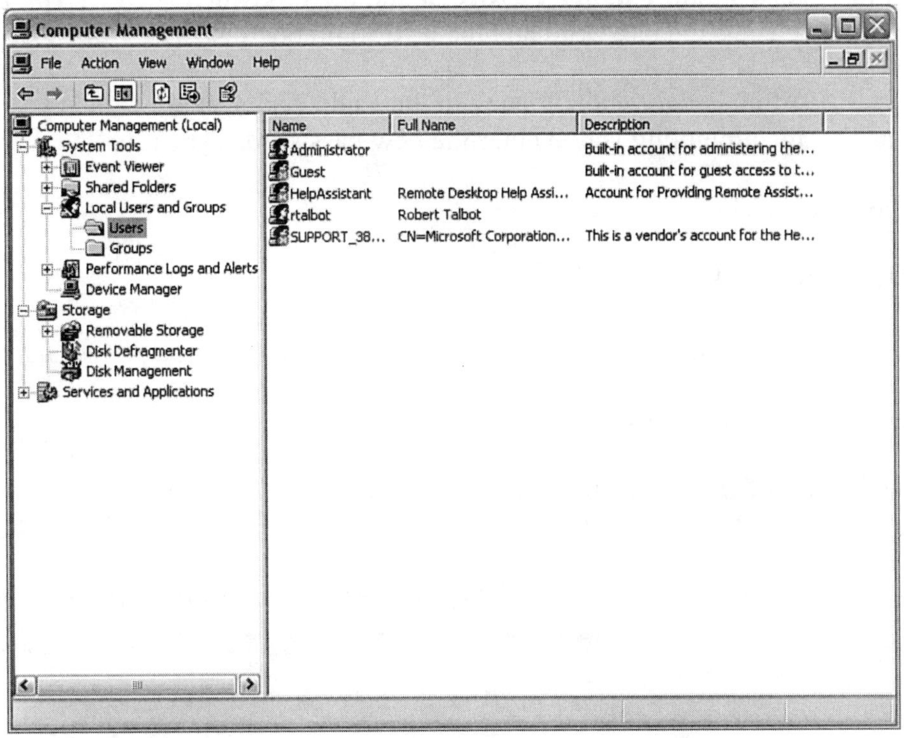

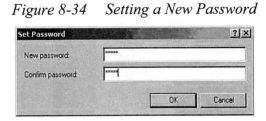

5. Right-click the **studentA1** account and select **Properties**.

6. Select the **User Cannot Change Password** and the **Password Never Expires** radio buttons. Then, click **OK**.

Step 2: Changing a Password

1. Right-click the **studentA1** account and click **Set Password**. Type in a new password and then type it again to confirm the password, as shown in Figure 8-34.

Figure 8-34   Setting a New Password

Step 3: Resetting a User's Password

1. Right-click the **studentA1** account and select **Properties**.

2. Deselect the **User Cannot Change Password** and the **Password Never Expires** radio buttons. The User must change the password and the next login box displays. Click **OK** to exit.

3. Log off as the Administrator and log on with the studentA1 account. When you log on, you receive a message prompting you to enter the new password. Type it in and then confirm it.

4 .Log off as studentA1.

Step 4: Deleting an Account

1. Open the Computer Management screen from Administrative Tools in the Start Menu.

2. Navigate to the studentA1 account.

3. Right-click the **studentA1** account and select **Delete**. Read the message and select **Yes** to confirm the delete user message (see Figure 8-35).

Figure 8-35   Deleting a User Account Confirmation Page

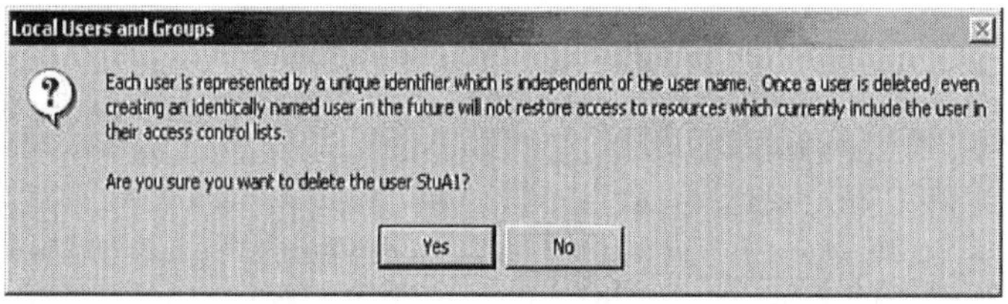

Troubleshooting

Sometimes, a user will have problems with their account. Passwords can be forgotten or entered incorrectly, and after a certain number of attempts ,a user can be locked out. You can use these tasks to unlock the account. User account management should be kept simple to maintain the large number of user accounts in a large company.

Worksheet 8.3.2: User Accounts

1. Before logging on to any Windows 2000 client, a _____ must first be created on the appropriate network server.

2. The task of creating an account in Windows 2000 is performed with the _____ tool.

3. The User name is a required field, must be no longer than 20 characters in length, and cannot contain the following symbols: _____

4. The simplest user management technique is to right-click the username listed in the right half of the Computer Management window and select the appropriate task from the menu. From here, the system administrator can instantly choose to _____, _____, or _____ the user.

Lab 8.4.1: Creating Files and Directories Using Windows 2000

Estimated Time: 15 Minutes

Objective

In this lab, you learn how to create files and directories in Windows 2000.

Equipment

The following equipment is required for this exercise:

- Computer system running Windows 2000 Professional

Scenario

The IT department in your company purchased some new computer systems. They want you to create new directories and files on the server for the people that are going to be receiving these new computers.

Procedures

In the first step of this lab, you create a directory or folder. In the second step of the lab, you create a file and save it inside the directory.

Step 1: Creating a Directory

1. Log in using the Administrator account.

2. Right-click the **My Computer** icon, or the **Start** button, and select **Explore**.

3. Locate the Local Disk (C:) and click the plus sign (+) to expand this drive.

4. Click the **Local Disk (C:)** icon to display the contents of this drive on the right side of the Windows Explorer screen.

5. Move the cursor to the right side of this screen, right-click in an open area, and select **New** > **Folder** to create a new directory on this drive.

6. When the folder is created, name it Lab5.3.5.

Step 2: Creating a File

1. Double-click the **Lab5.3.5** folder.

2. Right-click an open space in the directory and select **New** > **Text Document** to create a new file on this drive.

3. When the file is created, name the file Lab5.3.5document.

4. You can now open the file and continue to edit it or save it. Double-click the file to open it and then type the following:

   I have learned how to create a file and directories with Windows 2000.

5. Close the document and select **Yes** when you are asked if you want to save the file.

Troubleshooting

Make sure that filenames contain valid characters. There are some characters that Windows will not allow in a file or folder name. Do not use the following characters:

\ /: *? " < > |

Lab 8.4.2: Creating Groups in Windows 2000

Estimated Time: 20 Minutes

Objective

In this lab, you create groups in Windows 2000, add members to these groups, and organize user accounts.

Equipment

The following equipment is required for this exercise:

- System running Windows 2000 Professional

Scenario

The ABC Company stores sales reports on its Windows 2000 computer. The company wants to allow specific users to access these reports over the network. Your task is to create and configure the necessary groups to accommodate this request.

Procedures

A group is a collection of user accounts. Groups simplify the management of users and access to shared resources. Groups allow you to define permissions for multiple users at one time. After group permissions are defined, members are added to the group. Windows 2000 provides different types of groups for different tasks.

In this lab, you create two local groups, Marketing and Engineering. Next, you create the LocalUser1, LocalUser2, LocalUser3, and LocalUser4. You add users to the Engineering group and then remove a user from the Engineering group.

Note: The student account was deleted in Lab 8.3.2

Step 1: Creating Local Groups

1. Make sure that you are logged onto your computer as Administrator.

2. Create the following accounts: LocalUser1, LocalUser2, LocalUser3, and LocalUser4. Give each account a full name and make the password for each account, password.

3. Open the Computer Management screen by clicking **Administrative Tools** in the Start menu.

4 .Click the plus sign (+) to expand Local Users and Groups, and click **Groups**. displays the list of current and built-in local groups in the details pane.

5. To create a new group, right-click **Groups** and click **New Group**. The New Group dialog box appears.

6. Type **Marketing** in the Group Name box, and type **Access to Client Files** in the Description box. Click **Add**.

7. The Select Users Or Groups dialog box displays.

8. You need to scroll down the list of users to find LocalUser1 and LocalUser3. Hold the **Ctrl** key down and select LocalUser1 and LocalUser3 and click **Add.** Click **OK**.

9. In the New Marketing Group dialog box, LocalUser1 and LocalUser3 are listed in the Members box. Click **Create**.

10. Windows 2000 creates the group and adds it to the list of users and groups. The New Group dialog box is still open and might block your view of the list of users and groups.

11. Repeat Steps 5 through 10 to create a group named Engineering. Type **Access to design files** in the description box, and make LocalUser2 and LocalUser4 members of the Engineering group.

12. After you create both groups, click **Close** to close the New Group dialog box.

13. The Engineering and Marketing groups are listed in the details pane.

Step 2: Adding and Removing Members

1. In the details pane of Computer Management, double-click the **Engineering Group**.

   The Engineering Properties dialog box displays the properties of the group. LocalUser2 and LocalUser4 are listed in the Members box.

2. To add a member to the group, click **Add**. The Select Users Or Groups dialog box displays.

3. In the Name box, select LocalUser3, click **Add**, and then click **OK**.

4. The Engineering Properties dialog box lists LocalUser2, LocalUser3, and localUser4 in the Members box.

5. Select LocalUser4 and then click **Remove**.

6. LocalUser4 is no longer listed in the Members box. LocalUser4 still exists as a local user account, but it is no longer a member of the Engineering group.

7. Click **OK**.

Step3: Deleting a Local Group

1. Right-click the Engineering group in the Computer Management details pane and then click **Delete**.

> A Local Users and Groups dialog box appears asking whether you are sure that you want to delete the group.

> Click **Yes**.

> The Engineering group is no longer listed in the Computer Management details. The members of the group were not deleted. LocalUser2 and LocalUser3 are still local user accounts on the computer.

> Close Computer Management.

Troubleshooting

> You must be logged onto the system using an account with administrative privileges to perform system administrator tasks in Windows 2000. For this lab, make sure you are logged onto the computer using the Administrator account. If you experience any problems finding the necessary tools or making such changes to the system, make sure that you are first logged on as the Administrator.

Reflection

> What are some benefits of using groups to control access?

> _____
> _____
> _____
> _____
> _____
> _____

Lab 8.4.3: Assigning Permissions in Windows 2000

Estimated Time: 30 Minutes

Objective

In this lab, you learn how to assign NTFS permissions to the folders based on the scenario that is described in the following section.

Equipment

The following equipment is required for this exercise:

- Computer running Windows 2000 formatted with NTFS

Scenario

There is some material that contains sensitive data. It is your job as a system administrator to create the necessary folders and assign the proper permissions to these folders in order to protect the sensitive data. Your goal is to give LocalUser2 permissions to create and delete files in these folders and to prevent LocalUser1 from doing so.

Procedures

In the first part of the lab, you create the folders and assign permissions using the chart as a guide to help you create the folders and assign the proper permissions. You are asked to assign permissions to folders based on the following chart. Then, in the second part of the lab, you log in to the system and test these permissions that you created.

Step 1: Initial Lab Setup

You need to first create the folder structure on the C:\ drive of the hard drive of your computer exactly how it is shown in the following chart. The instructions to do so are as follows:

- Create a C:\Chemistry folder.
- Within the C:\Chemistry folder, create an Experiments folder and a Laboratory folder.
- Create a Week 3 folder in the Experiments folder.

The LocalUser1 and LocalUser2 user accounts should already be created. In the first part of the lab, you assign permissions to folders based on these folders and users that are created. You log on to the system as one of the users and test these NTFS permissions in the second part of the lab.

Folder	Users and Groups	Permissions
C:**Chemistry**	Users group → Administrators Group→	→ Read & Execute → Full Control
C:\Chemistry**Experiments**	Users group → Administrators Group →	→ Read & Execute → Full Control
C:\Chemistry\Experiments**Week_3**	Users group → Administrators Group → LocalUser2	→ Read & Execute → Full Control → Modify
C:\Chemistry**Laboratory**	Users group → Administrators Group →	→ Read & Execute → Full Control

Step 2: Verifying NTFS

Verify that you are logged in as Administrator. If you are not, log off and log back in as Administrator.

Open **My Computer** and right-click the **C:** drive.

Click **Properties**.

Under the General tab, verify that the file system is NTFS and click **OK**. If the file system is not NTFS, this lab will not work.

Step 3: Assigning NTFS Permissions for the Folders

Only the Administrator account can complete the following steps, so make sure that you are logged in with the Administrator account.

1. Open Windows Explorer and navigate to the Chemistry folder.

2. Right-click the **Chemistry** folder and select **Properties**. The properties box should be displayed for the folder in the General tab view as in Figure 8-36.

Figure 8-36   Folder Properties

3. Click the **Security** tab.

4. Next, click the **Add** button to add permissions for the user or group accounts according to the chart in Step 1.

Note: (You need to do this for each folder in the chart but you can do this for only one folder at a time.)

When you click the **Add** button, Windows displays the Select Users or Groups box, as shown in Figure 8-37.

Figure 8-37   Select Users and Groups Dialog Box

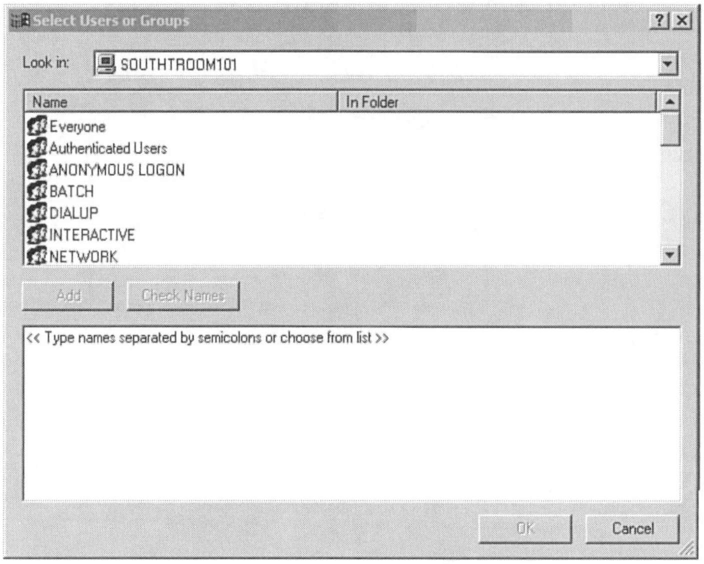

5. Make sure that the name of the computer in the computer box is your computer; if it is not, scroll through the drop-down menu and select your computer.

6. According to the chart in Step 1, begin adding user accounts and group accounts by selecting them in the name box and clicking the **Add** button. Again, do so according to the chart in Step 1; then click **OK**.

   Note: Do not proceed to Step 7 until all Users and Groups have been added to the specified folder according to the chart in Step 1.

7. To assign permissions, click the **users** group and set the permissions according to the chart in Step 1 by checking the appropriate box. You do this by right-clicking the folder and selecting the **Security** tab as in Steps 2, 3, and 4. Next, click the **admin** group and set the permissions by checking the appropriate box; click **Apply,** and **OK** to close the window.

You need to repeat Steps 6 and 7 for each folder that is highlighted in the chart in Step 1.

8. When you finish, click **OK** to return to the Properties dialog box for the folder.

9. Now, go back to the Chemistry folder and open the properties box by right-clicking the folder and selecting **Properties**. Then, select the **Security** tab again. If the Properties box contains user accounts and groups that are not listed in the chart, you need to remove them by selecting them; then click **Remove**. The Everyone group must be removed; otherwise, it will inherit the

permissions. To remove the Everyone group, deselect the box next to **Allow Inheritable permissions from parent to propagate to this object**. A warning message appears. Read it first and then select **Remove** to confirm that you want to remove the Everyone group. The Everyone group should automatically be removed at this point. (*Note*: If it isn't, manually remove the Everyone group by selecting it and clicking **Remove**.)

10. Click **OK** to save your changes and close the Properties box.

11. Close all the boxes and log off Windows.

Step 3: Testing the NTFS Permissions You Assigned in Step 1

1. Test the permissions for the Week 3 folder while logged on as LocalUser1.

- Log on as LocalUser1 and navigate to the Chemistry\Experiments\Week 3 folder.
- Try to create a file in the Week 3 folder.

Were you able to create this file?

2. Test the permissions for the Week 3 folder while logged in as LocalUser2.

- Log off Windows and log back on as LocalUser2; then navigate to the Chemistry\Experiments\Week 3 folder.
- Try to create a file in the Week 3 folder.

Were you able to create this file?

3. Test permissions for the Laboratory folder while logged in as Administrator.

- Log off Windows and log back on as Administrator; then navigate to the Chemistry\Laboratory folder.
- Try to create a file in the Experiments folder.

Were you able to create this folder?

4. Test permissions for the Experiments folder while logged in as LocalUser1.

- Log off Windows and log back on as LocalUser1; then navigate to the Chemistry\ Experiments folder.
- Try to create a file in the Experiments folder.

Were you able to create this folder?

5. Test permissions for the Laboratory folder while logged in as LocalUser2.

- Log off Windows and log back in as Local User2; then navigate back to the Chemistry\ Laboratory folder.

- Try to create a file in the Experiments folder.

Were you able to create this file?

Reflection

You can see from how you assigned permissions in this lab that you can control who has access to specific folders on a computer and how to protect sensitive files that are located on computers on a network.

Troubleshooting

Assigning NTFS permissions can be a confusing task when you work with large amounts of data. It is a good idea to keep the process as simple as possible. Also, when you format a drive or volume with NTFS, the Full Control permission is assigned to the Everyone group. You should change this default permission and assign other appropriate NTFS permissions to control access to the folders and files on the network.

Lab 8.5.1: Configuring HTTP Services on Windows 2000

Estimated Time: 30 Minutes

Objective

In this lab, you configure a Windows 2000 system with HTTP services and create a HTTP server.

Equipment

The following equipment is required for this exercise:

- Computer system running Windows 2000 Professional

Scenario

The Marketing Director of the XYZ Company asked you to create an HTTP site (website) that the employees in the marketing and sales department can access to provide content and information to their clients. It is your job to create an HTTP site on the server for them to access.

Procedures

In the first step of this lab, start the HTTP services and configure the HTTP site on the server. In the second step, configure the HTTP site properties and build the content that will be on the HTTP server.

Step 1: Starting the HTTP Services

1. Log on with the Administrator account.

2. Open the Control Panel. Go to **Start** > **Settings** > **Control Panel**.

3. From the Control Panel, double-click the **Add/Remove Programs** icon.

4. Next, click the **Add/Remove Windows Components** button.

5. When the Windows Components Wizard appears, as shown in Figure 8-38, click in the box next to **Internet Information Services (IIS)**.0

Figure 8-38   Windows Components

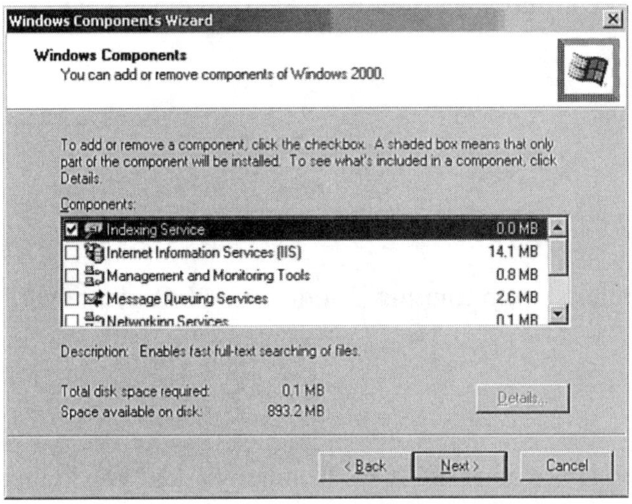

6. Click the **Next** button to install the Internet Information Services (IIS). You need the Windows 2000 CD to complete the installation. When prompted, insert the Windows 2000 CD to copy the necessary files. The installation process completes in a few minutes.

7. Click **Finish** to close the Installation box. Then, click **Close** to close the Add/Remove Programs Box and close the Control Panel.

Step 2: Configuring the HTTP Sites' Properties and Building the Content

1. Open the Start Menu and go to **Programs** > **Administrative Tools** > **Internet Services Manager**. This opens the IIS configuration page where you can begin to configure and create your HTTP site (see Figure 8-39).

Figure 8-39   Internet Information Services

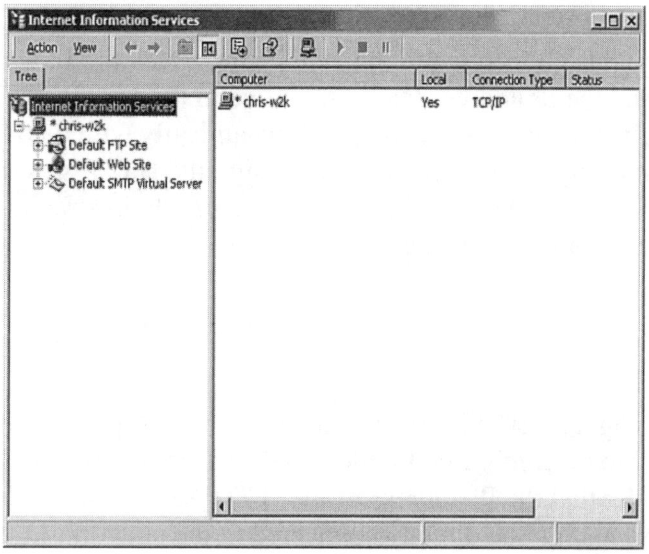

2. After the IIS page opens, find the name of your computer and click the plus (+) sign next to it. This displays the FTP, HTTP, and SMTP Virtual Server icons.

3. Click the **Default Web Site** icon to display the default website contents and the directories where the content files are stored.

4. Right-click the **Default Web Site** icon and choose **Properties**. From this page, you can configure all the properties and control what displays on your HTTP site.

5. While on the Web site tab, select the IP address box. Click the arrow from the drop-down menu and select the IP address of your computer.

6. Next, go to the **Connections** section of the same tab and change the **time-out** value to 120. After making these changes, select **Apply**.

7. Click the **Home Directory** tab and click **Browse** to select the folder that contains your website documents. This is typically C:\inetpub\wwwroot. Then, click **Apply** to save the changes. Close the Internet Services Manager.

Note: If you are using a third-party HTML editor such as FrontPage, you need to make your home directory folder the My Webs folder. As you create and edit your web pages, all the files will be saved in this folder, not the default folder.

To check if your HTTP site is working properly, go to any computer on the network and type the IP address of your HTTP server into the address bar of the Internet browser. You should see all the contents of your FTP directory in the browser.

Troubleshooting

If you have trouble connecting to the HTTP site, check the IP address that is typed in the browser and the IP address that is specified in the HTTP site properties page. If your network's IP addresses are assigned dynamically with a DHCP server, the IP address might change from time to time. Assign the HTTP server a static IP address so that the IP address does not change. This saves administrative overhead and trouble-shooting access to the HTTP site.

Reflection

If you are setting up a HTTP server in a business or corporate network, routers and firewalls need to be configured to allow HTTP access to the HTTP server. You also need to consider that the IP address of the HTTP server might not be a public IP address and, therefore, will not be directly connected to the network. In this case, you need to configure the router to forward incoming HTTP requests to the proper computer on which your HTTP server resides.

Lab 8.5.2: Configuring FTP Services on Windows 2000

Estimated Time: 20 Minutes

Objective

In this lab, you configure a Windows 2000 system with FTP services and create a FTP server.

Equipment

The following equipment is required for this exercise:

- Computer system running Windows 2000 Professional

Scenario

The marketing director of the XYZ Company wants you to create an FTP site that the employees in the marketing and sales department can access so that they can download files when they are away from the office. It is your job to create an FTP site on the server for them to access.

Procedures

In the first step of this lab, you start the IIS services and configure the FTP site on the server. In the second step, you configure the FTP site properties and build the content that will be on the FTP server.

Step 1: Starting the FTP Services

Note: The IIS services were installed when the HTTP server lab was complete. If not, complete Steps 1 through 6. If IIS services are installed, you can skip Steps 1 through 6.

1. Open the Control Panel. Click **Start** > **Settings** > **Control Panel**.

2. Double-click the **Add/Remove Programs** icon.

3. Next, click the **Add/Remove Windows Components** button.

4. When the Windows Components Wizard appears, click in the box next to **Internet Information Services (IIS)**.

5. Click the **Next** button to install the Internet Information Services (IIS). You need to have the Windows 2000 CD to complete the installation. When prompted, insert the Windows 2000 CD to copy the necessary files. The installation process will complete in a few minutes.

6. After the installation completes, click **Finish** to close the Installation box. Click **Close** to close the Add/Remove Programs box and close the Control Panel.

Step 2: Configuring the FTP Site' Properties and Building the Content

1. Open the Start Menu and go to **Programs** > **Administrative Tools** > **Internet Services Manger**. This opens the IIS configuration page where you can begin to configure and create your FTP site.

2. After the IIS page is open, find the name of your computer and click the plus sign (+) next to it. This displays the FTP, HTTP, and SMTP Virtual Server icons (see Figure 8-40).

Figure 8-40   Internet Information Services

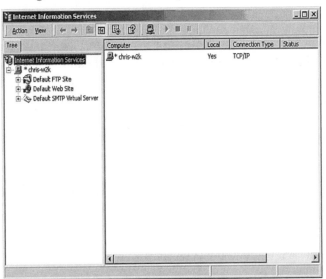

3. Right-click the **Default FTP Site** icon and select **Properties**.

4. From this page, you can configure all the properties and control what displays on your FTP site.

5. While on the FTP site tab, go to the IP address box and select the IP address of your computer from the drop-down menu.

6. Go to the Connection section of the same tab and change the value from 10 to 2 to limit the number of connections to allow at a time. Then, change the **time-out** value to 120. After making these changes, select **Apply**.

7. Next, select the **Messages** tab and create messages that will display to users when they connect to your FTP server.

8. Click the **Home Directory** tab and click **Browse** to select the folder that will be used when the FTP site is accessed. Click **OK** to save the changes and close the Internet Services Manager.

9. Go to the C:\Inetpub\ftpdata directory. Right-click and create a small text file. Save this file as MyFTP.

   Note: Make sure that the content of this folder contains only the information and files that you want on your FTP server.

10. Verify that your FTP site is working at the command prompt. Go to **Start** > **Run** and type **cmd.exe**. At the command prompt in Figure 8-41, type in your IP address (ftp 10.1.1.5, for example).

   • Log in as **anonymous** and press **enter** for the password.

   • Now type the word **dir** to see if the file MyFTP file is there.

   • Type the word **bye** to exit your FTP session.

Figure 8-41   FTP Command Prompt

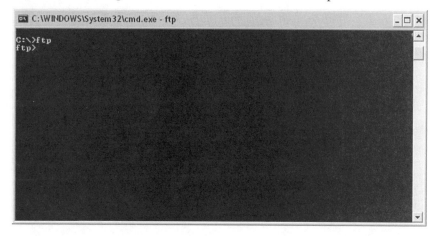

Troubleshooting

If you have trouble connecting to the FTP site, check the IP address that is typed in the browser and the IP address that is specified in the FTP site properties page. If your network's IP addresses are assigned dynamically with a DHCP server, the IP address might change from time to time. Assign the FTP server a static IP address so that the IP address does not change. This saves administrative overhead and troubleshooting access to the HTTP site.

Reflection

If you set up an FTP server in a business or corporate network, routers and firewalls need to be configured to allow FTP access to the FTP server. You also need to take into account that the IP address of the FTP server might not be a public IP address and, therefore, will not be directly connected to the network. In this case, you need to configure the router to forward incoming FTP requests to the proper computer on which your FTP server resides.

Lab 8.5.3: Configuring Telnet on Windows 2000

Estimated Time: 40 Minutes

Objective

In this lab, you configure Telnet services on Windows 2000.

Equipment

The following equipment is required for this exercise:

- System running Windows 2000 Professional

- Network connection from the workstation to a hub or switch

- PC with a Telnet client program connected to the same hub or switch

Scenario

The ABC Company installed a server running Windows 2000. The company wants you to configure Telnet services so that the workstation can be remotely administered using Telnet.

Procedures

Before beginning this lab, make sure that both the Windows 2000 workstation and the other PC are ready for you to log in. Power these hosts on, if necessary.

This activity requires that the PC connects to at least one other host on the same IP network. Verify that the Ethernet connections are in place. If you use a hub or switch, check the LED lights to verify that you have a connection.

Finally, ask your instructor or a lab technician for the appropriate IP address information for both hosts. Record that information in the tables provided:

Connected Host IP Address Configuration	
IP address:	
Subnet mask:	
Default gateway:	

Local Host IP Address Configuration	
IP address:	
Subnet mask:	
Default gateway:	

Record the IP address of the server and workstation in the boxes provided in the network diagram.

Step 1

After the Windows server boots, the Welcome to Windows dialog box appears. Log in as the Administrator.

Step 2

Configure the Windows 2000 workstation's IP address, subnet mask, and default gateway to match the information entered in the table. (This information might already be configured from a previous lab. If this is the case, get the other workstation's information.) Configure the workstation's IP stack accordingly. Use ping to verify that the server can communicate.

Step 3

On your workstation, start the Computer Management console. Go to **Start** > **Programs** > **Administrative Tools**.

Step 4

After the Computer Management window displays on screen, click the plus (+) symbol to the left of **Services and Applications** and select **Services** from the expanded tree as in Figure 8-42.

Figure 8-42   System Services

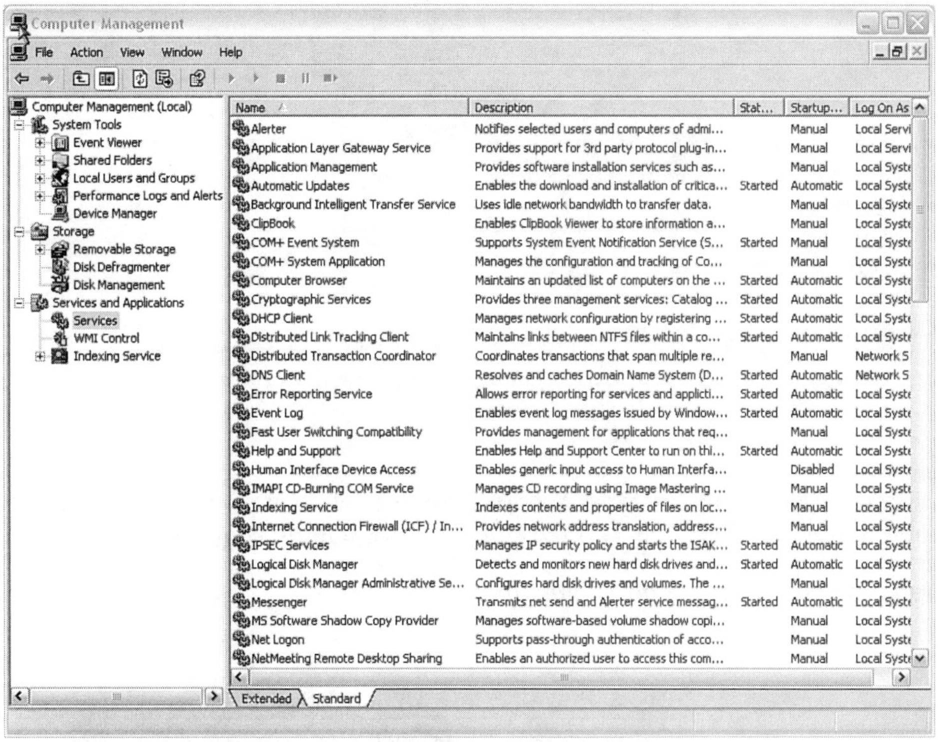

The Services section contains controls for starting and stopping the various services that are run in Windows 2000.

Step 5

To allow Telnet clients to connect to the workstation, the Telnet service must be started. Scroll the right pane until the Telnet service is visible.

The Status column is blank for the Telnet service indicating that the service is not currently running. To start the Telnet service, right-click the service and select **Start** from the menu as in Figure 8-43.

Figure 8-43   Enabling the Telnet Service

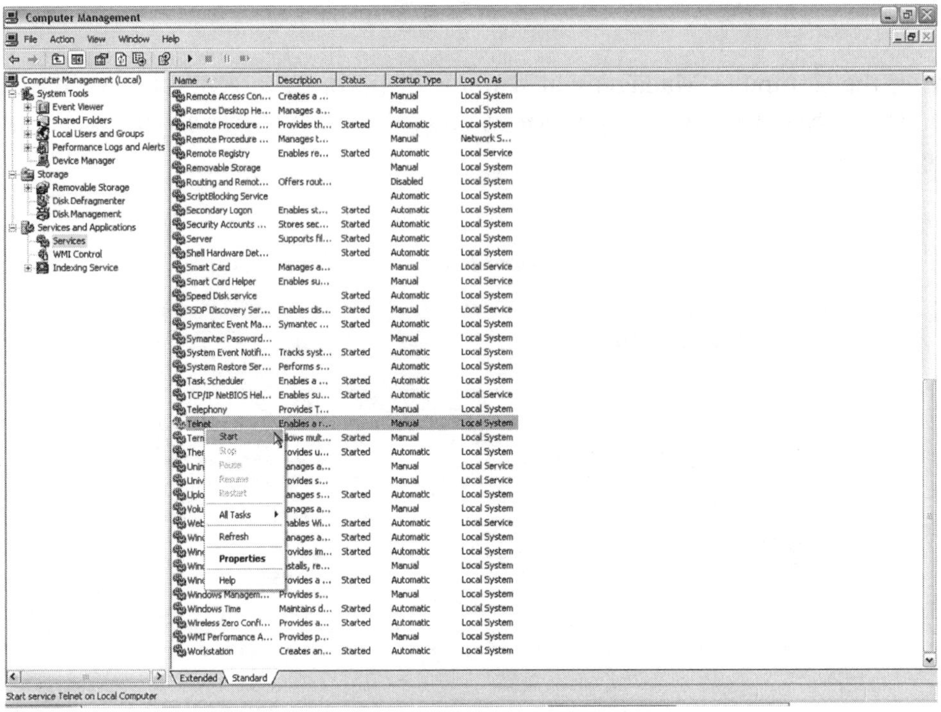

A Status indicator displays as Windows attempts to start the service. Check the Status column and verify that the service started, as shown in Figure 8-44.

Figure 8-44   Telnet Status Indicator

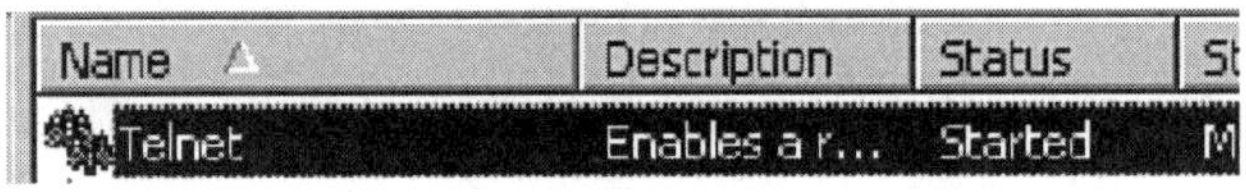

Step 6

The Telnet service for Windows 2000 defaults to using NTLM (NT LAN Manager) authentication, which is not supported on all systems. To make sure that the Telnet service works with any Telnet client, the service needs to be configured to accept clear text usernames and passwords if NTLM authentication fails. To do this, start Telnet Server Administration, which is located in the Administrative

Tools menu next to Computer Management. You should see the screen in Figure 8-45.

Figure 8-45   Telnet Windows

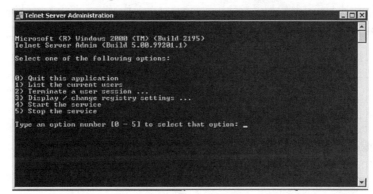

Step 7

The Telnet Server Administration program is a menu driven program to allow plain text and NTLM. Press **3** to enter the Display/Change registry settings section of the program. At the next menu, choose **7** for NTLM. The default value for NTLM is 2, which does not allow clear text authentication in any circumstances. Changing the NTLM value to 1 allows clear text authentication if NTLM fails. The following dialog with the menu changes NTLM to 1:

```
Current value of NTLM = 2

Do you want to change this value? [Y/n] y

NTLM [current value = 2; acceptable values 0, 1 or 2]: 1

Are you sure you want to set NTLM to: 1? [Y/n] y
```

Activate the changes that were just made by stopping and restarting the Telnet service.

Note: Although it is convenient to allow clear text authentication so that clients can have unrestricted access to the Telnet service (provided a valid username and password are present during the Telnet login), it is not recommended that you enable clear text authentication on a production server.

Step 8

To restart the Telnet service, enter a **0** to return to the main menu, and press the corresponding number **5** to stop the service. Verify that the Telnet service has stopped by going to Computer Management. After the service has been stopped, it can be started again by choosing the correct number **4** from the menu. The following text appears on the screen when the service is started:

```
Starting Microsoft Telnet Service...

Microsoft Telnet Service started successfully
```

The Telnet service can also be initially started from here and the Computer Management console. Now that the Telnet service has been started and configured on the Windows 2000 workstation that will be used to telnet into, the other workstation should be able to test the connection to it using a Telnet client.

Use the **netstat –a** command to verify connections.

Step 9

Go to another workstation and test this connection. On the workstation, the easiest way to start a Telnet session to the Windows 2000 server is to go to **Start** > **Run** and enter **telnet** *ip_address_or_hostname*. For the example in Figure 8-46, the IP address is 192.168.0.4.

Figure 8-46   Telnet from the Run window

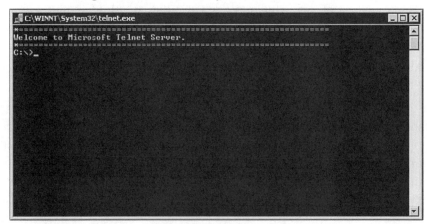

After the Telnet client window displays, it might warn you that you are about to send password information through the Internet zone and it will prompt you for permission. Click **Yes**, and the window in Figure 8-47 displays.

Figure 8-47   Successful Telnet Connection

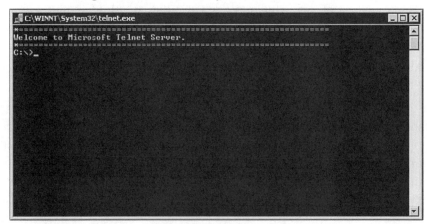

A Telnet session is comparable to having a command prompt open on the Windows 2000 server; and from here, the system can be manipulated remotely.

Note: The current logged in user (name and password) on the local computer will be used automatically when establishing a Telnet session. If the user is not defined on the Telnet destination computer, you need to provide a valid login name and password.

Step 10

In some environments, the statistics of the computer you are logging into might not always be known. There are some commands and programs that can give useful information about the server you are logged in to. Among these is the **ver** command, which displays the version of windows that the system is running. Type **ver** into the Telnet window and press **Enter**. Output similar to the following should be displayed:

```
C:\>ver


Microsoft Windows 2000 [Version 5.00.2195]


C:\>
```

The **netstat -a** command is also useful in tracking connections to the server, as the results in Figure 8-48 demonstrate.

Figure 8-48   **netstat -a** *Command*

While logged in to the server, you can run programs and issue commands, provided that they do not require the GUI.

When you finish with your Telnet session, type **exit** at the command prompt. **Exit** will end your Telnet session.

Troubleshooting

This lab requires that the two workstations have TCP/IP connectivity with each other. If you cannot telnet to the server from the workstation, verify each system's IP configuration and physical connections to the network.

If the Telnet session is opened, but you cannot log in, verify that the username and password you are using have been configured on the server.

Also, verify that you disabled NTLM authentication, as described in Step 6 of this lab.

Reflection

1. Telnet allows administrators remote access to the server. What kind of administrative tasks can you perform using the Windows CLI with Telnet?

_____

_____

_____

2. Telnet service is not enabled by default on a Windows 2000 server. What are the dangers of enabling Telnet services?

_____

_____

_____

_____

Lab 8.5.6: Writing a Script in Windows 2000

Estimated Time: 30 Minutes

Objective

In this lab, you learn how to write a script in Windows 2000.

Equipment

The following equipment is required for this exercise:

- Computer running Windows 2000 Professional

Scenario

You want to create a script in the startup folder that will display on the users' desktops when they log onto their systems. To experiment with writing scripts for that, you practice with a sample script that you will be creating in this lab.

Procedures

In this lab, you create and execute a Visual Basic Script and place it in the Start Menu.

Step 1: Writing the Script

1. Open up Notepad. Go to **Start** > **Programs** > **Accessories** > **Notepad**.

2. Type this text into Notepad:

```
Dim Greeting
Dim UserName


UserName = InputBox ("Please enter your name:")


UserName = Trim (UserName)
If UserName = "" Then
  Greeting = "Why won't you tell me your name? That's not very nice."
ElseIf UserName = "go away" Then
  Greeting = "That's not very nice."
ElseIf Username = "who's asking?" Then
  Greeting = "I asked you first."
Else
  Greeting = "Hello, " & UserName & ", it's a pleasure to meet you."

  If UserName = "Steve" Then
    Greeting = Greeting & " I like the name Steve."
  End IF
End IF


MsgBox Greeting
```

3. Save the document as Greeting.vbs.

> *Note*: If you need to edit changes after saving, change the extension to .txt.
>
> To change the file back to a .vbs script, go to the following folder:
>
> C:\WINNT\system32
>
> In this folder, associate the Greeting.vbs file with the wscript file.

Step 2: Executing the Script

1. Navigate to the folder where you saved the file and double-click it.

2. Do not type anything in the box and click **OK**. Notice what message is displayed and how it corresponds to the entry in the text of the script.

3. Click **OK**.

4. Double-click the script again and this time type **go away** in the box. Notice what message is displayed and how it corresponds to the entry in the text of the script.

5. Click **OK**.

6. Double-click the script again and this time type **who's asking** in the box. Notice what message is displayed and how it corresponds to the entry in the text of the script.

7. Click **OK**.

8. Double-click the script again and this time type **Alice** in the box. Notice what message is displayed and how it corresponds to the entry in the text of the script.

9. Click **OK**.

10. Double-click the script again and this time type **Steve** in the box. Notice what message is displayed and how it corresponds to the entry in the text of the script.

Step 3: Executing the Script When the System Starts

1. Navigate to your Startup folder. Go to C:/Document and Settings/All Users/Start Menu/ Programs/Startup. Drag the script file that was created in Step 1 and place it into the folder.

2. Restart your computer and the script should execute automatically when your system reboots.

Troubleshooting

Troubleshooting a Visual Basic Script or any script can be difficult because the text has to be 100 percent accurate for the script to execute properly. Review the script before it is saved and executed to make sure that is written correctly.

Reflection

Scripts can serve a variety of functions and can be helpful to a system administrator. The script that was written in this lab was a fairly simple script compared to how complex a Visual Basic script can be.

1. What are some other uses for scripts?

2. Where might they be useful and where might they cause harm?

Lab 9.2.1: Installation of Linux

Estimated Time: 50 Minutes

Objective

In this lab, you install the Red Hat distribution of Linux, configure the Linux settings as needed, and create a boot disk.

Equipment

The following equipment and documentation is required for this exercise:

- Red Hat Linux CDs
- Extra floppy disk
- PC hardware inventory documentation
- Linux documentation

Procedures

In this lab, the Linux operating system will be installed on a computer where the hard drive has been formatted and no operating system exists. Also, the BIOS has been set to allow the CD-ROM to boot the computer.

Many companies have created different distributions of Linux. The Linux kernel remains the same among these distributions, but the different versions appeal to different markets. In this lab, you use the Red Hat distribution of Linux version 7.2.

Step 1: Setting the BIOS Settings

The Linux CD is capable of booting the computer. Before starting the installation process, be sure that the BIOS settings are set to boot the computer from the CD-ROM (see Figure 9-1).

Note: Your BIOS setting might look different than the BIOS setting of this particular PC.

Figure 9-1   *BIOS Settings*

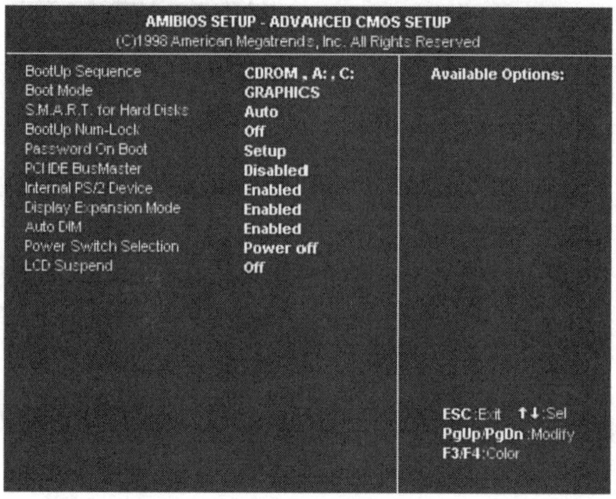

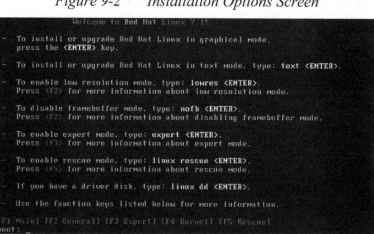

Step 2: Installation Options, Graphical or Text Mode

Place the Red Hat CD in the computer and turn on the computer. On boot up, this screen opens first. To install Linux in the graphical mode, press the **Enter** key and Linux takes you to the next screen (see Figure 9-2). If you do not press the Enter key in approximately thirty seconds, Linux starts the installation process in the graphical mode.

Figure 9-2   *Installation Options Screen*

Step 3: Language Selection

English is the default language for the Linux installation. The language you select in Figure 9-3 helps Red Hat find a time zone later in the installation process.

Select the appropriate language and click the **Next** button.

Figure 9-3   Language Selection Screen

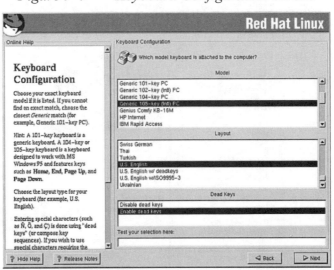

Step 4: Keyboard Configuration

Red Hat auto detects your keyboard. If you want to choose another keyboard, select the correct model here. If you cannot find an exact match, choose a **Generic** one.

The default Red Hat keyboard layout is English; choose another layout if needed.

Dead keys allow the creation of special characters with multiple keystrokes (such as Ñ, Ô, and Ç). Dead keys are enabled by default, but if you do not need them, select **Disable dead keys**.

To test your keyboard, use the blank text field at the bottom of the screen in Figure 9-4. When you finish selecting the keyboard options in Figure 9-4, click the **Next** button to continue.

Figure 9-4   Keyboard Configuration Screen

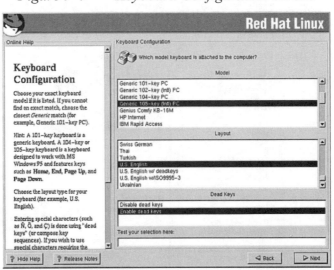

Step 5: Mouse Configuration

Red Hat auto detects your mouse; most of the time, you simply need to read this screen and click the **Next** button. Be sure to check the **Emulate 3 Buttons** checkbox.

If you choose to use another type of mouse, select it from the screen in Figure 9-5. Select a mouse type that you are sure is compatible with your system, if you cannot find an exact match.

If you cannot find a mouse that is compatible with your system, select one of the **Generic** options.

Figure 9-5   Mouse Configuration Screen

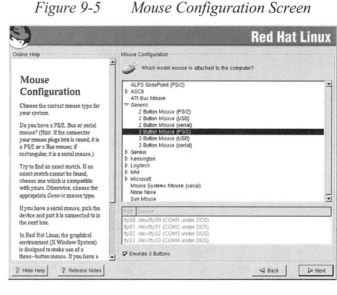

Step 6: Welcome to Red Hat Linux

The Welcome screen is for informational purposes only. Read the help text in the left panel for instructions and for information to register Red Hat (see Figure 9-6). After you read this screen, click the **Next** button.

Figure 9-6   Welcome to Linux System Installer Screen

Step 7: Install Options

Read the installation options text and select the Custom installation (see Figure 9-7). Click the **Next** button.

Figure 9-7   Installation Options Screen

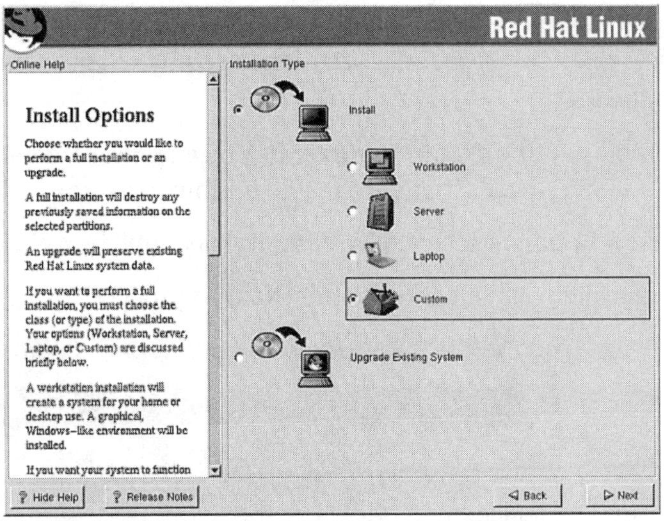

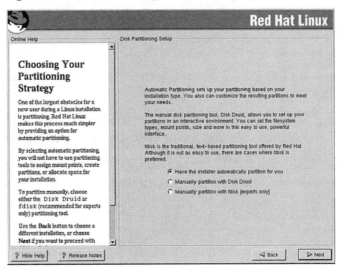

Step 8: Disk Partitioning

Partitioning divides the hard drive into sections that work as individual hard drives.

On the screen in Figure 9-8, you can choose to perform automatic partitioning, partition manually using **Disk Druid**, or partition manually using the DOS utility **fdisk**.

For this installation, select the **Automatic** partitioning option and Red Hat automatically partitions the hard drive.

After you select the automatic partition option, click the **Next** button.

Figure 9-8   Choosing Partitioning Options Screen

Step 9: Automatic Partitioning

As displayed in Figure 9-9, the automatic partitioning options are as follows:

- **Remove all Linux partitions on this system**—Removes existing Linux partitions and leaves other partitions intact. Select this option for this lab.

- **Remove all partitions on this system**—Removes all partitions on your hard drive, which might include partitions used by other operating systems such as Windows 9x.

- **Keep all partitions and use existing free space**—Keeps your partitions and uses the free space (if any) to create a Linux partition.

The **Review** option is selected by default; leave this box checked.

After you make your selections, click **Next** to proceed.

Figure 9-9   Automatic Partitioning Options Screen

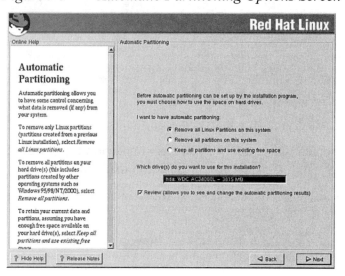

Step 10: Partitioning Your System

The screen in Figure 9-10 displays how Red Hat automatically determined the hard drive setup.

Note: Red Hat creates three partitions: one for the Linux Kernel (/boot), one for the files and applications (/), and a swap file to store data that does not fit into RAM.

You have the option to edit the settings. For the purpose of this lab, accept the default settings and click the **Next** button.

Figure 9-10   Partitions Screen

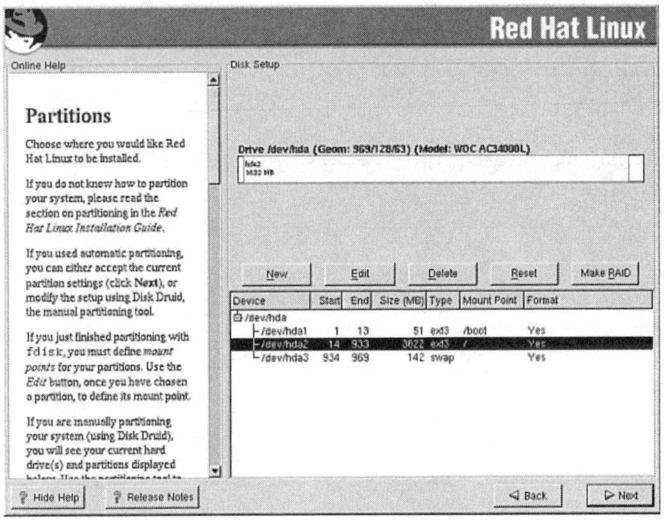

Step 11: Boot Loader Installation

Linux needs a boot loader to help the computer find the operating system. Boot loaders are usually installed in the Master Boot Record (MBR). GRUB is a relatively new boot loader, but for the purpose of this lab, the Linux Loader (LILO) boot loader should be selected. Be sure to select the settings as shown in Figure 9-11:

- Use LILO as the boot loader.

- Install Boot Loader record on /dev/had.

- Boot label: Linux.

After you review the settings, click the **Next** button.

Figure 9-11   Boot Loader Selection Screen

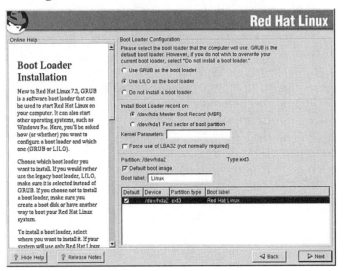

Step 12: **Network Configuration**

The default setting for the network interface card (NIC) is to use the Dynamic Host Configuration Protocol (DHCP) settings. Change this by clicking the **Active on boot** checkbox.

Ask your instructor for the correct settings. At a minimum, enter in the following information:

IP Address	
Netmask	
Host name	
Gateway	

If you are given more settings, such as Network, DNS, Broadcast, and so on, they also can be entered.

The screen in Figure 9-12 is only an example; ask your instructor for the correct data.

Review the settings and click the **Next** button.

Figure 9-12   Network Configuration Screen

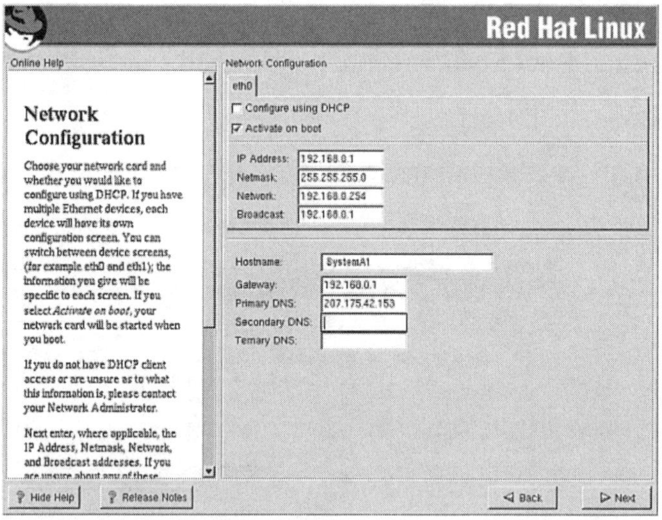

Step 13: Firewall Configuration

When you reach this point, select the **No Firewall** option and be sure to select all the boxes next to **allow incoming**, that is, **DHCP**, **SSH**, **Telnet**, **WWW (HTTP)**, **Mail (SMTP)**, and **FTP**.

Security level settings:

The **High** selection allows only the following connections:

- DNS replies

- DHCP

The **Medium** selection does not allow the following:

- Ports lower than 1023, such as **FTP**, **SSH**, **telnet**, and **HTTP**, are blocked.

The **No firewall** disables any security checking.

Choose **Customize** to add trusted devices or to allow additional incoming services.

The **Trusted devices** selection allows access to your system for all traffic from that device. It excludes that device from any firewall rules.

In later labs, you connect to other computers in your classroom and use network protocols such as FTP and HTTP to connect to those computers. Click the **Customize** button and check the **eth0** box under the Trusted devices, as shown in Figure 9-13.

Review the selections and click the **Next** button.

Figure 9-13   Firewall Configuration Screen

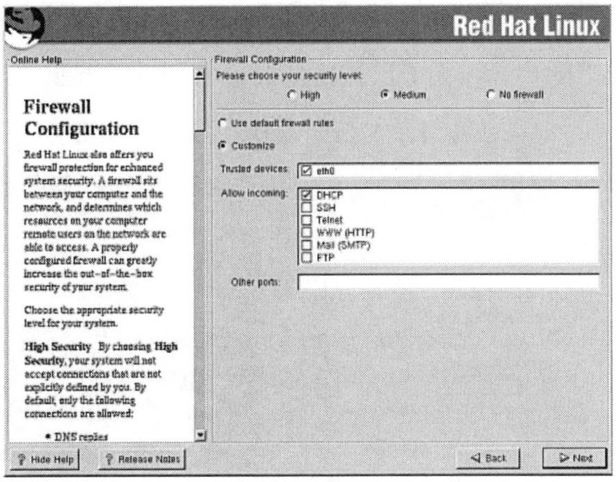

Step 14: Language Support

Choose a language that will be used as the default on your Linux system. If you choose to install other languages, you can change your default language after the installation. Installing too many languages can take up too much hard drive space.

After you select a language from the screen in Figure 9-14, click the **Next** button.

Figure 9-14   Language Support Screen

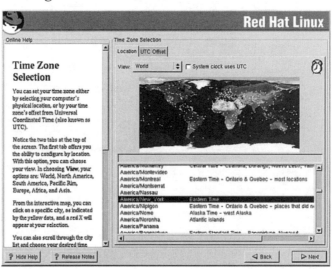

Step 15: Time Zone Selection

Select the correct time zone by scrolling to and highlighting the correct city from the screen in Figure 9-15. Click the **Next** button when finished.

Figure 9-15   Time Zone Selection Screen

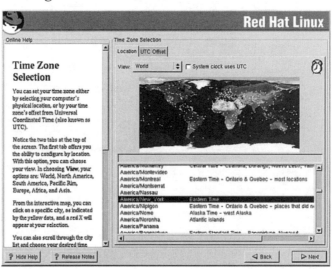

Step 16: Account Configuration

Enter the root password twice:

Root Password: **cisco1**

Confirm: **cisco1**

Create a new user with the **Add** button, as shown in Figure 9-16. Ask your instructor for the correct name and password.

Figure 9-16   User Account Configuration Screen

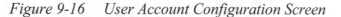

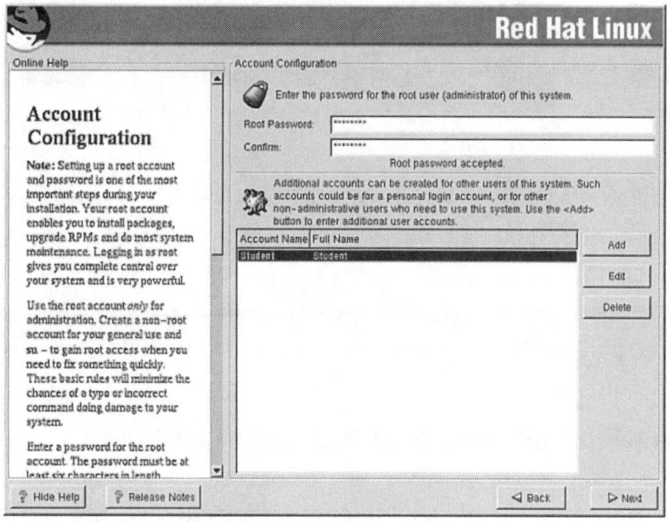

In the **Add a New User** box, as shown in Figure 9-17, enter the following information:

- **User Name**—The name the student will use to log in to the system.

- **Full Name**—The complete name of the student.

- **Password**—Enter a password the student or user can log on with initially.

- **Confirm**—Re-enter the password for confirmation.

Figure 9-17   Configuring Additional Accounts

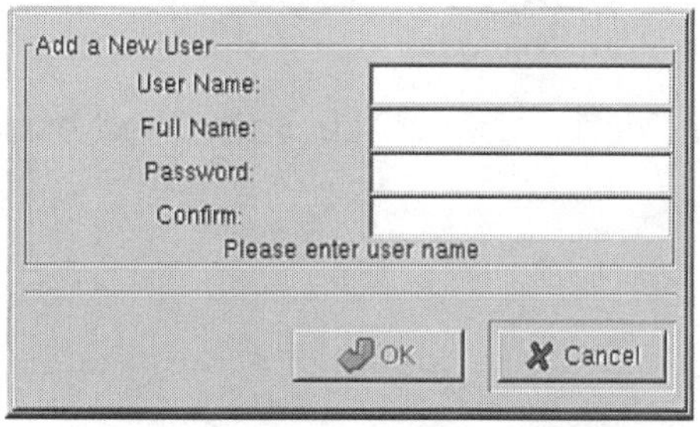

Step 17: Authentication Configuration

Read the screen in Figure 9-18 and press the **Next** button.

Figure 9-18   Authentication Configuration Screen

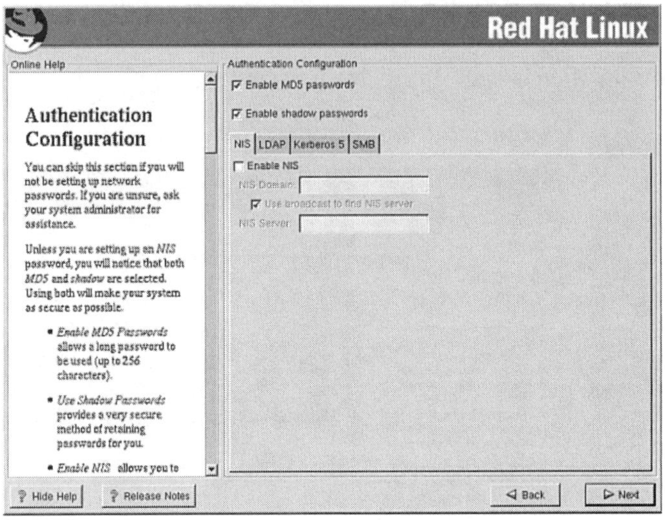

Step 18: Selecting Packages and Groups

It is important that you do not select the default settings.

Make sure that the following boxes, as shown in Figure 9-19, are checked:

- ✓ Printing Support
- ✓ Classic X Windows System
- ✓ X Window System
- ✓ GNOME
- ✓ KDE
- ✓ Sound and Multimedia Support
- ✓ Network Support

Do not choose the everything option, because your hard drive has not been portioned with enough space.

After selecting the correct boxes, click the **Next** button.

Figure 9-19   Package Selection Screen

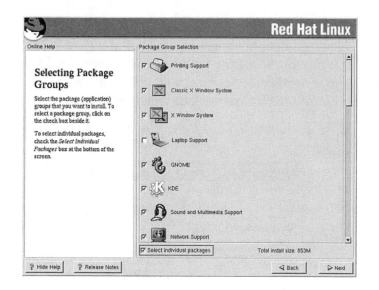

Step 19: Unresolved Dependencies

Software libraries must be installed before they can function properly. Red Hat checks your system for all the required libraries. Red Hat Linux checks for these dependencies each time you install or remove software packages. If Red Hat finds any errors, it locates the correct dependencies and installs them.

Read the display, as shown in Figure 9-20, and click the **Next** button.

Figure 9-20   Unresolved Dependencies Screen

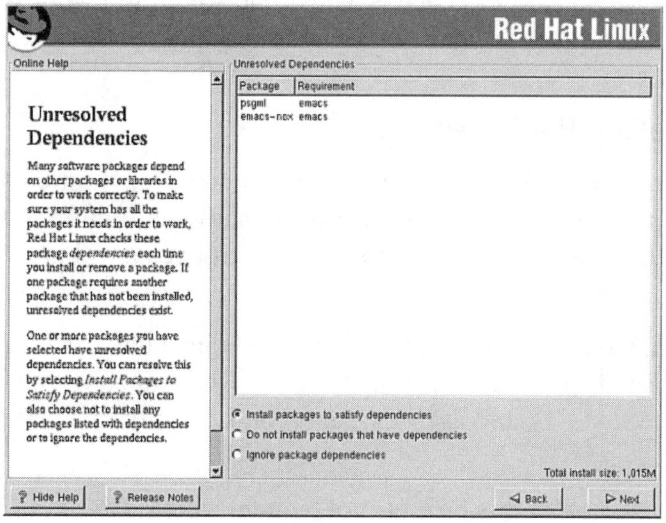

Step 20: Video Configuration

Red Hat auto detects your video card.

If your video card does not appear on the list in Figure 9-21, X Windows might not support it. You can choose the **Unlisted Card** option and attempt to configure it by matching your card's video chipset with one of the available X servers. Ask your instructor for information about your video card.

Figure 9-21   Video Card Configuration Screen

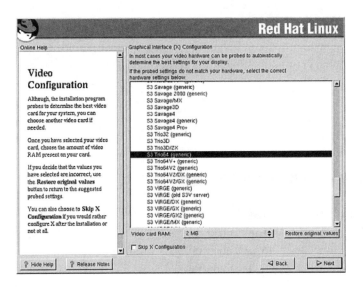

Step 21: Preparing to Install

After the video card has been selected, the About to Install screen displays. There are no selections to be made on this screen. Read the information and click the **Next** button.

Step 22: Installing Packages

Red Hat installs all the necessary software to set up your computer. There are no selections to be made during the process shown in Figure 9-22. How long this process takes is dependant on the number of packages being installed and the speed of the computer.

Depending on the number of packages to be installed, you might be asked for the second Red Hat CD-ROM. If this occurs, Red Hat stops the installation process, ejects the first CD, and asks for the second. Simply insert the second disk and press **Enter**.

It is important that this process not be interrupted. Do not turn the power off or reset the computer—if this happens you have to start over.

Figure 9-22   Package Installation Screen

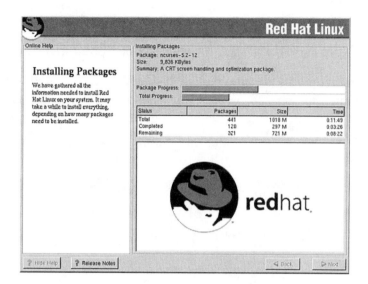

Step 23: Boot Disk Creation

After the software packages are installed, you will be asked to create a boot disk, as shown in Figure 9-23. If your system cannot boot, a boot disk can bypass the LILO boot loader and you can start the computer with the floppy disk.

Install a blank floppy disk and Linux creates the boot disk. After the disk has been created, remove it and be sure to label it.

Figure 9-23   Boot Disk Creation Screen

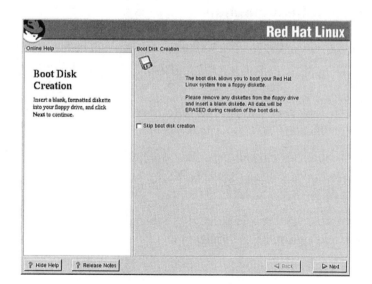

Step 24: Configuration

Usually, Red Hat auto detects your monitor. If your monitor was automatically found, it will be listed in the screen, as shown in Figure 9-24. Click the **Next** button.

If your monitor was not auto detected, select a Generic model from the list. If a Generic monitor is selected, Red Hat will suggest horizontal and vertical sync ranges. After your settings have been selected, click the **Next** button.

Figure 9-24   Monitor Selection Screen

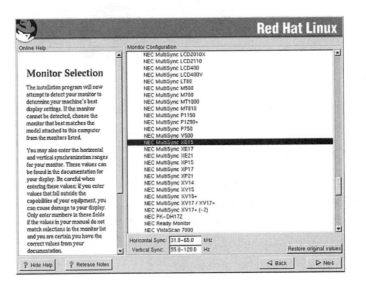

Step 25: Custom X Configuration

From the screen in Figure 9-25, choose the correct color depth and resolution for your X configuration. Click **Test Setting** to try out this configuration. If you do not like what you see during the test, click **No** to choose another resolution.

You need to test your configuration to make sure the resolution and color settings are usable.

Your desktop environment depends on whether you installed GNOME or KDE. If you installed both GNOME and KDE, you can choose which one to use as your default desktop environment.

For the purpose of this lab, select the KDE desktop environment. Additionally, select the text option as the login type.

Figure 9-25   X Server Configuration Screen

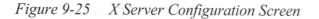

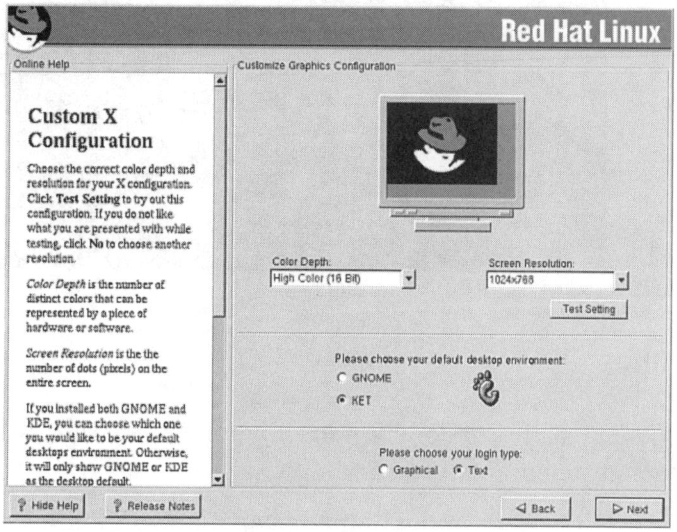

Step 26: Installation Complete and Booting Up for the First Time

Red Hat Linux 7.2 installation is now complete.

You will be prompted to prepare your system for reboot. Remove any diskette and CDs.

When the system is restarted, the screen in Figure 9-26 appears as the system boots up.

Figure 9-26   Linux Boot Screen

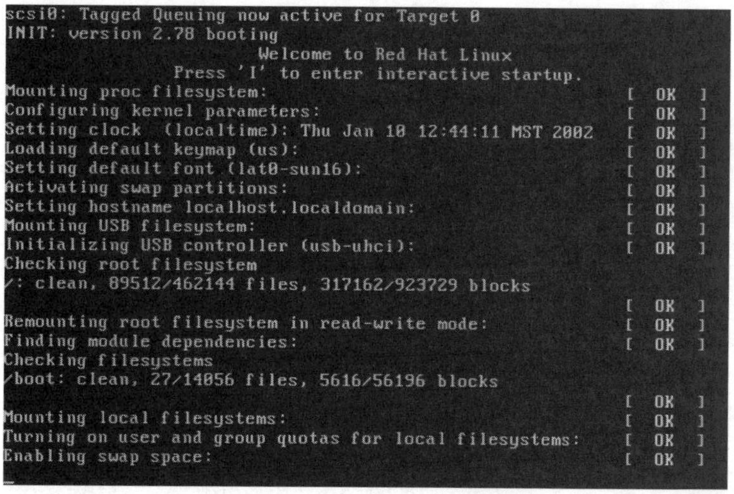

After the operating system has loaded you will be asked to log in, as shown in Figure 9-27. At this point, you can stop. Logging in and starting the KDE interface are discussed in the next lab.

Figure 9-27   Linux Login Screen

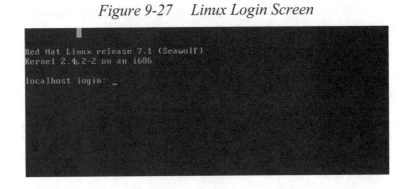

Troubleshooting

The following is a list of common installation problems. List possible solutions below each installation problem.

1. The computer won't boot from the Linux installation CD-ROM.

_____

_____

2. Linux did not find the video card or my monitor.

_____

_____

3. LILO did not load and the computer did not boot up.

_____

_____

Reflection

1. What are the advantages to installing LILO on a floppy disk and booting the computer from the floppy desk?

_____

_____

2. When should firewalls be enabled and when should they be disabled?

_____

_____

3. When should Linux be configured to go directly into X Windows on boot up?

_____

_____

Lab 9.2.3: Configuring Network Settings

Objective

In this lab, you configure a Red Hat 7.2 Linux computer's IP address.

Equipment

The following equipment is required for this exercise:

- Computer server with Linux Red Hat 7.2 installed
- Network connection from the server to hub, switch, or some other host

Scenario

The Air Guitar Company purchased a server with Linux Red Hat 7.2 installed. The company asked you to configure the server with an IP address and subnet mask.

Procedures

Before beginning this lab, make sure that the Red Hat Linux system is ready for you to log in. Ask your instructor or a lab technician for the appropriate static IP address information for your server. Record that information in the table provided Answers will vary based upon IP address configuration of the classroom:

Server IP Address Configuration	
IP address:	
Subnet mask:	
Default gateway:	

Note: The IP address, Subnet mask, and Default gateway in this lab are only examples. Ask your instructor for the IP scheme used in your lab and write them down in the preceding table. Refer to this table and not to the following examples for the correct IP addresses.

Step 1: Log in as root

In this lab, you change the network IP address. In the Linux system, only the root account can configure an IP address.

1. Log in as the root user.

   If you are in the GUI, open a terminal window. (Click the **terminal emulator** icon on the bottom of the screen to open the terminal window.) Configure the IP address and subnet mask using the command-line interface (CLI).

Step 2: ifconfig

IP addresses are assigned to physical interfaces, such as Ethernet NICs. IP addresses can also be assigned to logical interfaces, such as a local loopback. An interface typically has only one IP address assigned to it; although, it is possible to assign more than one IP address to an interface.

Configure an interface's IP address using the **ifconfig** program. The "if" in ifconfig stands for interface.

Use the **man** command to get information on the ifconfig program; type the following:

```
man ifconfig
```

1. According to the man output, when are you likely to use **ifconfig**?

   _____

2. According to the man output, what does the **ifconfig –a** option do?

   _____

3. Type **q** to exit the **man** page.

   From the shell prompt, run the **ifconfig** program with the **–a** option; type the following:

   ```
   ifconfig -a
   ```

   Note: All TCP/IP hosts associate the IP address 127.0.0.1 as a loopback address. In the output preceding, you see that the loopback interface "lo" has the 127.0.0.1 address, with a mask of 255.0.0.0. Although you can use **ifconfig** to change the loopback's IP address, it is recommended that this address not be changed.

   Notice how Linux refers to your Ethernet NIC. The output that you see might be different from the preceding sample. In this exercise, the NIC is referenced as **eth0**. If the interface that you are configuring has a different designation, be sure to substitute your interface name for **eth0** in these examples.

Your Ethernet NIC (eth0) might already have an IP address bound to it. The **ifconfig** program displays IP addresses and their associated masks, as shown in Figure 9-28:

Figure 9-28   **ifconfig** *Command Screen*

The "inet" stands for Internet (IP) Address. The word "Mask" refers to the IP Subnet Mask.

4. What is the **HWaddr** of your computer's NIC (s)?

5. What does **HWaddr** stand for?

Step 3: Configuring the IP address

Use the **ifconfig** command to set up the Ethernet interface's IP address. Use the information that you wrote down in the table (see the "Procedures" section).

1. Enter the appropriate command at the shell prompt.

The following example is correct, given a new IP address of 192.168.0.5 and a subnet mask of 255.255.255.0. Type the following:

[root@systemA1 root]# **ifconfig eth0 192.168.0.5 netmask 255.255.255.0**

The **netmask** argument specifies the subnet mask. Verify that the change has taken effect by issuing the **ifconfig –a** command. IP address changes take effect immediately in Linux; you do not need to reboot the system.

The output of the **ifconfig –a** command (see Figure 9-29) should indicate that the new IP address is bound to the NIC. Type the following:

```
ifconfig -a
```

Figure 9-29 **ifconfig –a** *Command Screen*

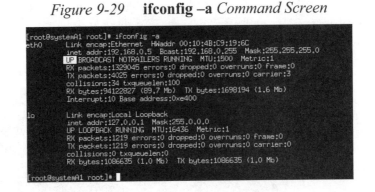

At this point, **ifconfig** should report this interface as UP, as shown by the high-lighted preceding output. If this interface shows down, troubleshoot the Ethernet connection. You must plug an Ethernet cable into the NIC and connect the other end to a networking device, such as a hub or switch.

You can manually bring down an interface by using the down argument (**ifconfig eth0 down**). To return a down interface to the UP state, use the **up** argument (**ifconfig eth0 up**).

Step 4: Ping Command

To test the configuration, you can use Internet Control Messaging Protocol (ICMP) (), better known as ping.

Use the **man** command to get information on the **ping** program, as shown:

```
man ping
```

Send a ping to your own interface. Use **CTRL-C** to stop the pinging. The following example assumes that you have configured the interface as 192.168.0.5. Type the following:

```
ping 192.168.0.5
```

```
PING 192.168.0.5 (192.168.0.5) from 192.168.0.5: 56(84) bytes of data.
64 bytes from 192.168.0.5: icmp_seq=0 ttl=255 time=240 usec
64 bytes from 192.168.0.5: icmp_seq=1 ttl=255 time=108 usec
64 bytes from 192.168.0.5: icmp_seq=2 ttl=255 time=136 usec
64 bytes from 192.168.0.5: icmp_seq=3 ttl=255 time=133 usec
64 bytes from 192.168.0.5: icmp_seq=4 ttl=255 time=135 usec
64 bytes from 192.168.0.5: icmp_seq=5 ttl=255 time=132 usec
64 bytes from 192.168.0.5: icmp_seq=6 ttl=255 time=136 usec
64 bytes from 192.168.0.5: icmp_seq=7 ttl=255 time=131 usec
64 bytes from 192.168.0.5: icmp_seq=8 ttl=255 time=136 usec

--- 192.168.0.5 ping statistics ---
9 packets transmitted, 9 packets received, 0% packet loss
round-trip min/avg/max/mdev = 0.108/0.143/0.240/0.035 ms
```

In the preceding output example, 64 bytes from 192.168.0.5 means that a reply of 64 bytes was received from that host. If you do not receive a reply, you might have typed the wrong IP address, either with the **ping** command or when you used **ifconfig**.

Remember to ping your own IP address and to use CTRL+C to stop the continuous pings.

If other hosts are connected to your network, try pinging them. You need to ask to find out what their addresses are. A successful ping reply from another host means that your IP configuration is working and that you are live on the network.

Step 5: Router Command

For the server to communicate with TCP/IP hosts beyond the local subnet, the system must use the services of a local router. The term gateway was commonly used in the past to refer to a router because a router acts as a gateway to other networks. When configuring a host for IP, you might also need to configure its *default gateway*, which is the IP address of the local router's interface.

In the Linux CLI, you can manually configure the default gateway using the **route** program.

Use the **man** command to get information on the **route** program, as shown; type the following:

```
man route
```

1. According to the **man** output, what is the primary use of the **route** program?

_____

2. What does the **–n** switch do when it is added to the router command?

_____

Check your system's route table; type

```
route -n
```

to get the results similar to Figure 9-30.

Figure 9-30 **route –a** *Command Screen*

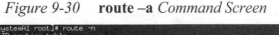

Your system might already have a default route to the gateway installed. The preceding output shows that the kernel's routing table knows no default route. That means this host cannot send messages beyond its local subnet, 192.168.0.0/24.

You can use the route program to install a default route to the gateway (the router). The following example installs 192.168.0.1 as the default gateway:

Use the information recorded in the table (from Step 3) to install a default gateway on your system. Replace the highlighted address in Figure 9-31 with the address appropriate to your network. Type in the following command at the # prompt:

```
route add -net 192.168.0.1
```

Figure 9-31 **route add –net** *Display*

```
[root@systemA1 root]# route add -net default gw 192.168.0.1 dev eth0
```

If you are adding a default route and the route already exists, you will receive the following error message:

```
SIOCADDRT: File exists
```

If directed by your instructor, use another IP address for the default gateway.

When you are done, use **route** to check the modified routing table (see Figure 9-32); type the following

```
route -n
```

Figure 9-32 **route –n** *command*

```
[root@systemA1 root]# route -n
Kernel IP routing table
Destination     Gateway         Genmask         Flags Metric Ref    Use Iface
192.168.0.0     0.0.0.0         255.255.255.0   U     0      0        0 eth0
127.0.0.0       0.0.0.0         255.0.0.0       U     0      0        0 lo
0.0.0.0         192.168.0.1     0.0.0.0         UG    0      0        0 eth0
[root@systemA1 root]#
```

Step 6: Reboot

Reboot your system using the **reboot** command.

Return to the CLI; nd use **ifconfig** and **route** to display your current IP addressing configuration. You should notice that any changes you made in previous steps using those commands have disappeared.

The system should be configured just as it was before you began the lab. This is because the ifconfig command that you ran does not change the startup config files that Linux uses to configure the NIC.

Manually using the ifconfig and route programs every time the system boots would not be an inefficient way to configure IP addressing information. Fortunately, Linux runs several scripts during boot time, some of which perform the task of IP address configuration. You can modify the script files manually with a text editor or use a program to modify these files for you. After these scripts are correctly configured, your system reboots with the desired IP configuration.

The easiest way to modify the relevant script is to use the **netconfig** program.

At the shell prompt, run the **netconfig** program, as shown; type the following:

```
[root@systemA1 root]# netconfig
```

The **netconfig** program presents you with a configuration dialog, as shown in Figure 9-33.

Figure 9-33 **netconfig** *command*

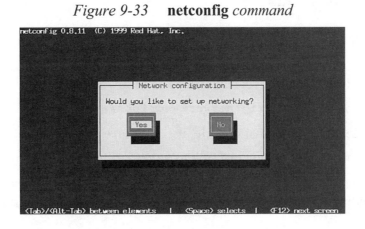

Based on your answers, the program configures the appropriate scripts for you. Select **Yes** to set up networking and continue on to the next screen in Figure 9-34.

Figure 9-34 **netconfig** *command*

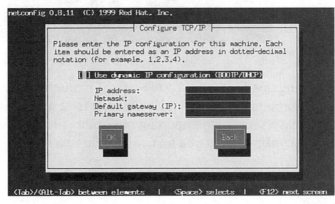

This final configuration screen gives you the option to configure TCP/IP. You can select dynamic configuration, which means that your system will query a DHCP or BOOTP server in an attempt to automatically configure its IP address. Dynamic IP addressing is used for workstations and desktop PCs.

Typically, servers are manually configured for a static IP address. If a server's address were to change from one day to the next, users and other systems might not be able to find them.

Enter the IP address, subnet mask, and default gateway information that you recorded in the table (Step 3). For now, you can leave the primary nameserver (DNS) field blank or allow the default address to remain in the field.

Use **ifconfig** and **route** to verify that your changes have taken immediate effect. Reboot the system and check again to make sure that these settings remain intact.

Step 7: Network Scripts

You can also modify the IP configuration script files manually using a text editor such as **vi**.

In Red Hat Linux, the relevant file is as follows:

`/etc/sysconfig/network-scripts/ifcfg-eth0`

To check the contents of this file, use the **more** command:

`more /etc/sysconfig/network-scripts/ifcfg-eth0`

Note: The highlighted portion in Figure 9-35 might be different on your system, depending on how your Ethernet NIC is designated by the kernel.

Figure 9-35   Network Interface Information

Manually editing this file (and then rebooting) is another way to change the IP address configuration of your NIC. However, it is easy to mistype a configuration command or leave something important out of this file. For these reasons, you should use **netconfig** instead of a text editor whenever possible.

Troubleshooting

As an IT professional, configuring and troubleshooting TCP/IP is typically a daily activity. A common problem with manually configured IP addresses is operator error. Always double-check a static IP configuration. Most operating systems warn you when they detect another node on the network with the same IP address.

Reflection

Administrators usually manually configure static addresses on servers. Why is static configuration uncommon among workstations?

Should a large company allow employees to manually assign IP addresses on their workstations? Why or why not?

_____
_____
_____
_____
_____
_____
_____

Lab 9.3.3: Configuring X Server

Estimated Time: 15 Minutes

Objective

In this lab, you learn to properly configure the X server GUI environment with the available tools.

Equipment

The following equipment is required for this exercise:

- Computer with Linux Red Hat 7.x installed

Scenario

You are the system administrator of a large company and you have recently installed Linux Red Hat on several systems. Some of the hardware that is installed in these systems requires that extra configuration be done to the X windows GUI.

Procedures

Step 1: Running the Xconfigurator Tool

The Xconfigurator tool can be used in either text mode or GUI mode. It depends from which mode it is launched. This goes through a series of menus that allows you to pick the appropriate settings. It is an easy and user-friendly tool. The next steps of this lab walk you through how to use the Xconfigurator tool.

1. Using the Xconfigurator command in Linux allows you to manually configure the X windows GUI. Type the following command at the shell prompt:

```
Xconfigurator
```

The Xconfigurator interface should display, as shown in Figure 9-36.

Figure 9-36   XConfigurator Interface

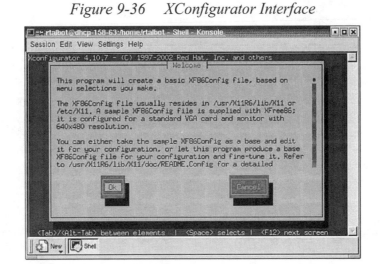

2. You will not be able to use your mouse. You need to use the Tab key on your keyboard to navigate through the menus. Press the **Tab** key until the **OK** button is selected and then press **Enter**.

The Xconfigurator interface should now display, as shown in Figure 9-37.

Figure 9-37   XConfigurator Interface

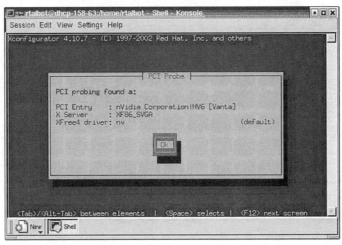

3. In this screen, the system is detecting which type of video card is installed in your system, the version of X Server that is installed, and what driver is installed. You should read over this information, verify that it is correct, and then press the **Enter** key on your keyboard.

The Xconfigurator interface should now display, as shown in Figure 9-38.

Figure 9-38   XConfigurator Interface

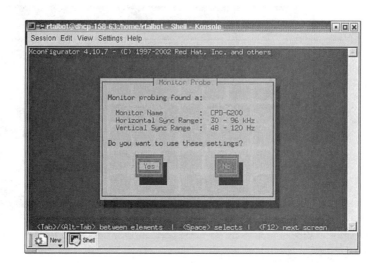

4. In this screen, the system is detecting which type of monitor is installed on your system. You should read over this information, verify that it is correct, and then press the **Enter** key on your keyboard to confirm these settings if they are correct.

The Xconfigurator interface should now display, as shown in Figure 9-39.

Figure 9-39   XConfigurator Interface

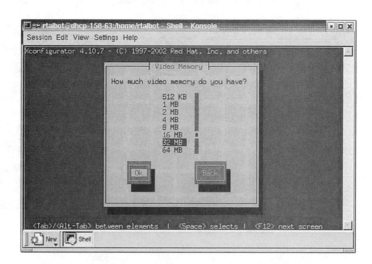

5. In this screen, the system is detecting how much RAM is installed on your video card. Most of the time, the system auto detects the amount of RAM. Use the up and down arrow keys to select the correct amount of RAM; then use the **Tab** key to select the **OK** button and press **Enter**.

The Xconfigurator interface should now be displayed, as shown in Figure 9-40.

Figure 9-40   XConfigurator Interface

6. In this screen, the system is detecting your clockchip configuration. It is recommend that you select the default option, which is **No Clockchip Setting**. Use the up and down arrow keys to select the correct setting; then use the **Tab** key to select the **OK** button and press **Enter**.

The Xconfigurator interface should now display, as shown in Figure 9-41.

Figure 9-41   XConfigurator Interface

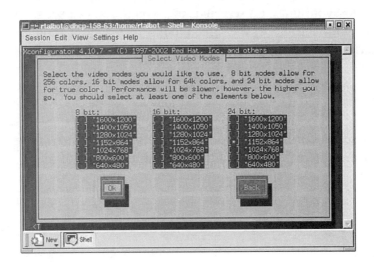

7. In this screen, you need to select the screen resolution size that you want. Again, use the **Tab** key to navigate around this screen. After you are at the location of the setting you want, press the **Spacebar** key on your keyboard to select it. Then, use the **Tab** key to navigate to the **OK** button and press **Enter**.

The Xconfigurator interface should now display, as shown in Figure 9-42.

Figure 9-42   XConfigurator Interface

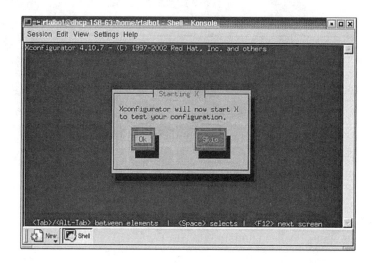

8. At this point, you have completed the configuration section. You will now proceed to the section in which you test and restart the X server with your new settings. To do this, make sure the **OK** key is selected and press **Enter**.

After you select **OK,** the screen flickers a few times and then you will be presented with a test configuration screen asking you if you can see the screen and if you want to accept the settings. If the screen looks okay—and it should if you configured properly—select **Yes**. The X server restarts and your new settings display.

Reflection

The X server configuration tools can be used only when you are logged in as the root user. Why is it important that regular users cannot run these tools?

Lab 9.4.1: Post-Installation of Applications and Programs

Estimated Time: 20 Minutes

Objective

In this lab, you install applications and programs after the installation of Linux Red Hat is complete.

Equipment

The following equipment is required for this exercise:

- Computer with Linux Red Hat 7.x installed

Scenario

You are the system administrator of a large company. You recently deployed several Linux Red Hat systems. You want all these systems to be installed with the latest version of the Netscape Navigator Internet browser. The version that comes with Linux when it is installed is not the latest version that is available, so you have to install it after the installation is complete.

Procedures

Step 1: Downloading the Package from the Internet

Note: Log in as the root user prior to starting this lab.

There are different ways to get the latest version of Netscape. One way is to get the CD, but for the purposes of this lab, you will download the package from Netscape's website.

1. Open the existing Netscape Communicator web browser that is installed and go to the Netscape homepage. To do this, click the **K start menu** > **Internet** > **Netscape Communicator** link. This opens the browser; then, click the **home** button. takes you to the Netscape homepage (www.home.netscape.com).

2. After the page loads, locate the **downloads** link on the top right corner and click it. This takes you to the page that lets you download the latest version.

3. At this screen, click the **free download** button.

4. After a couple seconds, the Save as box appears. You might want to note the location of where the file is being saved so that you can find it after it is installed. After you are ready, click **OK**. (Save in the default location and write down the path.)

Step 2: Unpacking and Installing the Application

1. Using the terminal Window, navigate to the folder where the application was saved. It should be your home folder. After you get to the directory where it is saved, type **ls -l** at the shell prompt. This lists the contents of the directory, and the file you downloaded should be in the directory. You should see the filename: **netscape-i686-pc-linux-gnu-installer.tar.gz**. That is the name of the file you need to unpack and install.

2. To unpack and install the file, enter the following command at the shell prompt:

   ```
   tar -xvzf netscape-i686-pc-linux-gnu-installer.tar.gz
   ```

   This should create a new directory called **netscape-installer** in the same directory. Use the **ls -l** command if you want to list the contents of the directory again.

3. Next, you need to change to the **netscape-installer** directory. To do this, enter the following command at the shell prompt:

   ```
   cd /netscape-installer
   ```

   Now, use the **ls -l** command to list the contents of the **netscape-installer** directory.

4. The next step is to enter the command to actually install the software. To do this, enter the following command at the shell prompt:

   ```
   /root/netscape-installer/netscape-installer
   ```

   This should automatically launch the Netscape installer window. Click **Next**; then, on the following screen, click **Accept** to accept the license agreement.

   Then, click **Next** again to accept the recommended installation.

   Note: Keep the default settings.

   On the next screen, click the **Install** button. It will take a few minutes for the files to download and install. After the status bar indicates that the download has completed, the software should self-install.

   After the installation has completed, you might get some boxes prompting you to register or to enter your Netscape username and password. You can do this if you want to or select **Cancel** and do it later—or not at all.

   After you hit **Cancel**, the new Netscape browser should open. When it does, close it.

Step 2: Using the New Application

1. Using the K-start menu, open the Netscape browser. To do this, click the **K start menu** > **Internet** > **Netscape Communicator** link. Notice that the old version of Netscape opened. This occurs in Linux because the old version of Netscape is still installed, and this link still points to the old Netscape version. You need to create a desktop application that links to the new version of Netscape.

2. To do this, right-click the desktop and select **Create new** > **Link to Application…**

3. The properties box opens. Type **Netscape** in the box and then click the **Execute** tab.

4. In the box, type the following:

   /usr/local/netscape/netscape

5. Next, click **OK**. Then, you can click your new desktop icon and launch the new Netscape browser.

Reflection

How does software installation in a Linux system compare to that in a Windows system? Are there any advantages to the way that it is done in a Linux system as opposed to a Windows system?

_____

_____

_____

_____

_____

_____

Lab 10.1.1: Logging In to Linux

Lab Time: 30 Minutes

Objective

In this lab, you boot a Linux computer and log in as the root user, navigate using the Command-Line Interface (CLI), and then shut down the computer.

This lab covers the following CLI commands:

- **su**
- **whoami**
- **man**
- **ls**
- **shutdown**

Equipment

The following equipment is required for this exercise:
- Computer with Linux Red Hat 7.2 installed

Scenario

You boot up the Linux computer and log in using the root user account. You run Linux in the command line mode and shut down the system using the UNIX-based shutdown command.

Step 1

Turn the computer on and observe the boot process. When Linux begins to load, you see the screen in Figure 10-1. This screen gives the user the option of booting into the text mode. Press the **Enter** key to bypass this screen or wait and Linux automatically begins to boot (approximately five seconds).

Figure 10-1   Linux Boot Screen

The boot process can take a few minutes. The time varies according to the speed of the computer. As Linux boots, the Linux processes loads. Your screen should look similar to Figure 10-2 as your Linux system boots up.

Can you make out any of these processes?

Figure 10-2   Processes Loading Screen

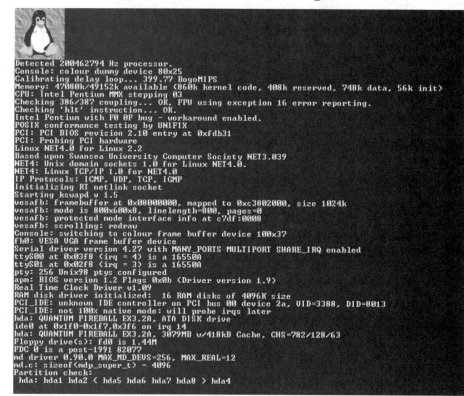

Step 2

After Linux is loaded, you will be prompted to log in. During the installation process, the CLI was set as the default boot. Figure 10-3 shows a CLI login prompt.

Figure 10-3   Login Screen

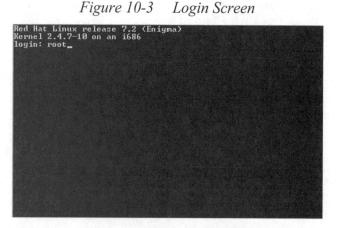

The Linux administrator account is called the root account. Type in **root** and press the **Enter** key. Be careful, like all UNIX computers, Linux is case-sensitive.

Next, type in root's password:

cisco1

Figure 10-4   Shell Prompt Screen

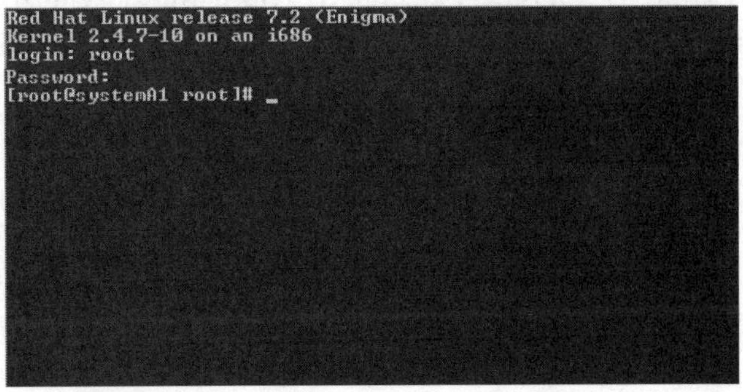

```
Red Hat Linux release 7.2 (Enigma)
Kernel 2.4.7-10 on an i686
login: root
Password:
[root@systemA1 root]# _
```

Note: The root account is signified by the # at the prompt.

Step 3

It is not a good practice to work as the root user. The root user has complete control of the Linux system, and you can inadvertently delete important files. It is better to work as a user that does not have total control and to switch to the root account only when maintaining or upgrading the system. In Linux, it is a simple process to switch users by using the **su** command.

During the installation process, two accounts were created: one for the root account and another account for general student use. Students need to ask the instructor for the student account name.

At the command prompt, type the following:

```
su - studentA1
```

Note: When the root user is switching users, they will not be prompted for a password; all other accounts will be prompted for a password.

Figure 10-5   **su** *Command*

```
[root@systemA1 root]# su - studentA1
[studentA1@systemA1 studentA1]$
```

Did the command prompt change? How?

Note: The "–" after the **su** command is called a *switch*. When switching users, this switch runs all associated user scripts. If you want to experiment, type **exit** after you log in as any user other than the root user. You end up back as the root user. Now type the following:

```
su studentA1
```

This time, try it without the "–" switch. What happened? Did you end up in studentA1's home directory?

Step 4

Make sure that you are logged in as a student user. To verify this, use the **whoami** command. The **whoami** command displays only the login name of the current user.

At the command prompt type in the following:

```
whoami
```

Figure 10-6 **whoami** *Command*

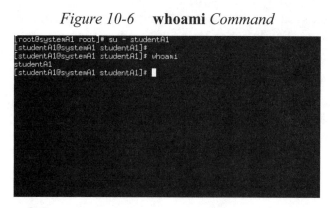

What were your results?

Step 5

Navigating the CLI is not difficult if you know where to find help. In Linux, the **man** command displays information about CLI commands.

For example, to learn about the **ls** command, type the following:

```
man ls
```

Figure 10-7 **man ls** *command*

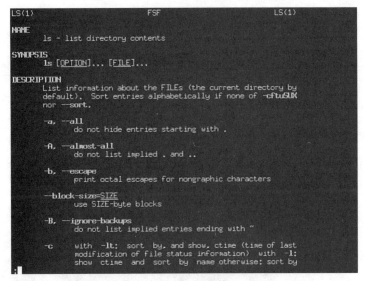

To move around the man screen, click the **Enter** key to move down.

Like DOS, Linux commands can have switches associated with them. The **ls** command uses many switches; **-a** and **–l** are the most common.

To exit the man command, type the following:

q

You return to the CLI.

Step 6

At the CLI, type in the following commands. Describe the results after each command is entered:

ls

ls -a

ls -al

Figure 10-8 **ls command** *Options*

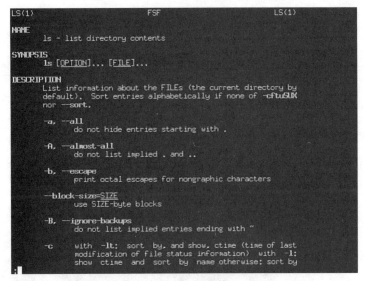

Can you tell from the preceding results how files are hidden in Linux?

Hint: What character does Linux place in front of the file to hide it?

Step 7

In this step, using the shutdown command turns off the computer. Linux, like all NOSs, must complete the shutdown process. Linux needs time to shut down so that it can put files where they belong. Turning off a Linux system quickly can result in files being lost and the corruption of vital configuration settings.

To learn about the **shutdown** command, type the following:

    man shutdown

Figure 10-9   **man shutdown** *Command*

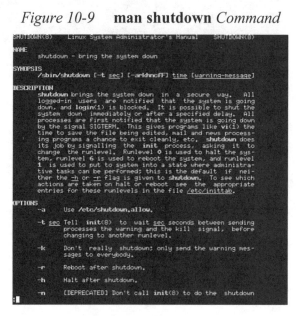

From this man page, briefly describe the **shutdown** command.

What does the **–r** switch do?

_____

_____

What does the **–h** switch do?

_____

_____

How is the time set with the **shutdown** command?

_____

_____

Remember, to exit the man help screen, type in the letter **q**.

Step 8

Only the root user is allowed to shut down a Linux computer. To complete this step, you need to verify that you are logged in as the root user. If you are not, type the following:

```
su - root
```

If requested, enter the root password.

Next, type the following:

```
shutdown -h now
```

Figure 10-10 **shutdown –h now** *Command*

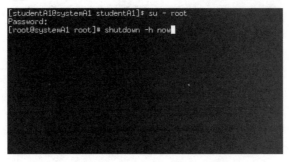

Describe the shutdown process.

_____

_____

_____

After the shutdown process completed, did the computer turn off? (*Note*: With an ATX power supply, it turns the computer off. Older AT boxes will not.)

Troubleshooting

As an IT professional, you might be asked to troubleshoot Linux login problems. Use the following list as a checklist when troubleshooting.

Problem: Cannot log in to the system

Possible causes:

- Username or password is misspelled or mistyped. Check both the username and password and carefully re-enter this information. In both Linux and UNIX, usernames and passwords are case-sensitive, so verify that the password uses the correct case.

- Keyboard CAPS LOCK is on. Press the **CAPS LOCK** key once, verify that the keyboard's CAPS LOCK indicator light is off, and try entering the password again.

- User has confused username with password. Verify that the user is typing his username in the User name field and his password in the Password field.

- When logging in through CLI, some users don't realize that although they do not see anything being entered as they type, the system is taking the input. It is sometimes common with beginning users to think their machine is frozen at this point.

Reflection

1. Why is it important to log out or lock the console when you leave it unattended?

_____

_____

2. What are some of the reasons a user might not be able to log in to the server?

_____

_____

_____

_____

3. What advantages does the ability to switch between multiple login terminals provide?

_____

_____

_____

_____

Lab 10.1.2: Using the Linux GUI (X Window)

Estimated Time: 25 Minutes

Objective

In this lab, you explore the basic features of the X Window and the KDE desktop environment.

Equipment

The following equipment is required for this exercise:

- Computer with Linux Red Hat 7.2 (or greater) installed

Scenario

The XYZ Company installed a server running Red Hat Linux 7.2. The company asks you to log in to the server with the administrative account. The server is configured with the KDE desktop environment. Your task is to explore the basic features of the KDE GUI.

Procedures

Before beginning this lab, power on or reboot the Red Hat Linux server.

Step 1: Starting an X Window Session

This Linux system was set up to boot into the command line by default. Linux, however, can be configured to boot into the GUI by default. If you are booting up your system, you need to log in and supply the password as you did in the previous lab. If you are already at the command prompt, type the following:

```
startx
```

The **startx** command initializes an X Window session and starts the KDE interface.

After the Red Hat Linux boots, the KDE Welcome dialog box appears. You do not need to log in to the GUI because you already supplied a username and password to authenticate yourself in the CLI.

Figure 10-11   Linux Terminal Window

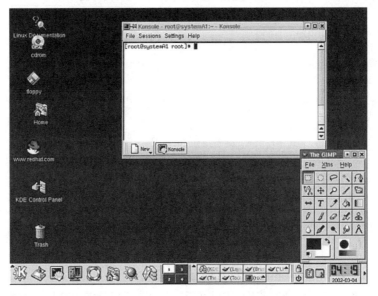

Step 2: Navigating the KDE Interface

After the system grants you access, you see your desktop environment on the server. The installation of Red Hat 7.2 allows you to install the KDE desktop environment. Use the KDE as the default GUI for all users. Other desktop environments, such as GNOME, can also be configured and used with Linux.

UNIX and Linux both rely on the X Window System to display the GUI. The X Window System is software that works with the system's hardware and graphical applications including the window manager. The window manager is the software responsible for sizing, positioning, and rendering the graphical windows that programs run in.

Windows include borders that can be dragged to resize and graphical buttons that can be clicked to minimize, maximize, restore, and close the window. Because Linux supports several window managers, and each window manager can be customized, there is no one way a window will look or act.

KDE, like most UNIX/Linux GUIs, is designed to use a three-button mouse. The function of each button can be customized on a per-user basis. The following table describes the functions commonly associated with each mouse button:

Mouse Button	Function
Left	Used to select and drag items.
Middle	Used to paste text or to move things
Right	Used to bring up a menu for the selected object (when applicable).

KDE is not a window manager; KDE can work with several different kinds of window managers. KDE is a desktop environment. A desktop environment is a combination of programs, applications, and applets that make up part of the GUI.

KDE provides the following:

- Graphical panels that can start applications or display status

- A graphical desktop that can place applications, files, and menus

- A standard set of desktop tools and applications

- A set of conventions that enable applications to work together consistently

After you log in, you see the KDE desktop. The panel contains icons that start key applications or open menus. It also contains a task bar that allows you to switch between running applications.

Figure 10-12 shows the icons that typically appear on the panel.

Figure 10-12   KDE Control Panel

The KDE desktop environment can be configured to look and act in many different ways. Some of KDE's key features can be configured using the KDE Control Center.

To switch to another desktop environment, go to the "K" at the lower-left corner of the screen. Hold the mouse down until the menu pops up and find the run command. Click the **run** command and type the following:

```
switchdesk
```

After you click **Enter,** you see a display of all the available desktops that are installed.

You do not want to switch to any other desktop environments at this time. Read the popup box and click **Cancel**.

Figure 10-13 **switchdesk** *Command*

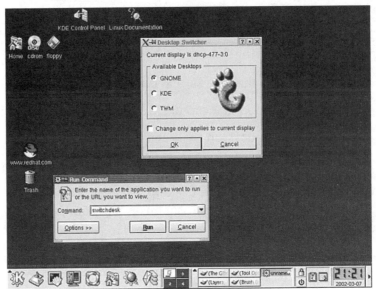

Run the KDE Control Center now by clicking once on the icon on the panel. The
KDE Control Center window appears, as shown in Figure 10-14.

Figure 10-14 KDE Control Center

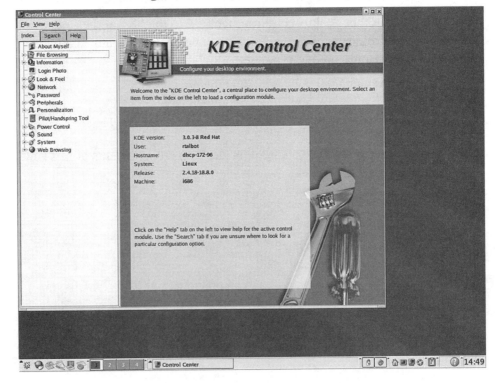

From the Control Center, you can customize aspects of KDE's appearance, including the desktop background, the window manager, and the panel.

Before leaving the Control Center, click the **Look and Feel** option under the Index tab. This gives you many options for configuring the KDE desktop environment.

The Look and Feel tool is the name of the window manager that KDE is working with. Remember, KDE can be configured to work with other window managers. There are many aspects of the window manager that you can configure here. For now, click the **Theme Manager** icon under the Look and Feel menu and then select the **Eclipse** option from the list, as shown in Figure 10-15.

Figure 10-15   KDE Theme Manager

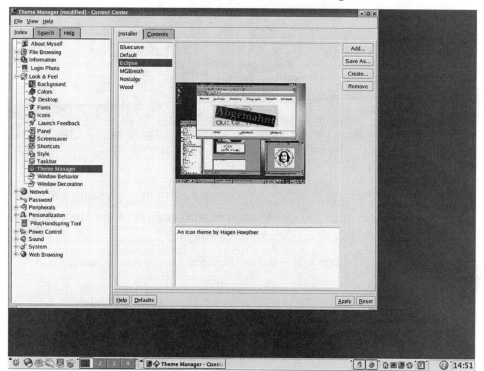

Click the **Apply** button at the bottom of the Control Center window. The new frame style should appear on all your open windows (see Figure 10-16). This change is purely cosmetic and does not affect the way the operating system functions.

Figure 10-16   KDE Desktop

To go back to the default KDE settings, reopen the KDE Control Center, click the **Look and Feel** button and the **Theme Manager**. Select the **Default** setting and click **Apply** and KDE reverts to its original settings.

Click the **X** at the top of the window to close the Theme Manager.

Step 3: Opening the Control Panel

Next, click the **KDE** start application button in the lower-left corner of the screen. A menu opens. Find the system menu (it will be about halfway up the menu) and drag the mouse up to it. After the mouse has been left there for a moment, a sub-menu opens up. Move the cursor up to the KDE Control Panel and click once.

Figure 10-17   Linux GUI Control Panel

In the KDE Control Panel, you must click the **Hardware Browser** icon (see Figure 10-18). If asked for the root password, enter it in the KDE dialog box that appears.

Figure 10-18   Hardware Browser

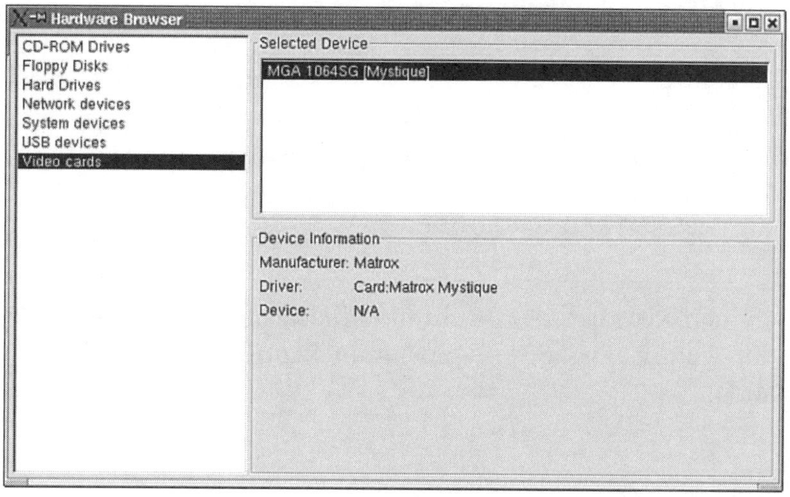

Click through each item listed. In the space below, briefly describe the disk information that is described under the Hard Drives section.

To exit the control panel, click the **X** in the upper-right corner of each window that is open.

Step 4: Closing X Window and Shutting Down the System

To close the X Window session entirely, close all the applications that are open. Next, click the following three keys simultaneously:

Ctrl + Alt + Backspace

This closes X Window and you are back in the CLI. You can also turn the computer off by typing the shutdown command in the CLI:

```
shutdown -h now
```

Or as an alternative, you can reboot the computer by typing the following:

```
shutdown -r now
```

Troubleshooting

Configuring X for a particular system can be a challenging task. Many software components are required, including a window manager and several libraries.

Problem: Cannot run X Window

Possible causes:

- Because X configuration can be complicated, you will need to consult websites and other documentation relevant to your software and your system. If you are in the CLI, try using the **ALT+F7** key combination to switch to X. If X is not running, type **startx** at the shell prompt.

Reflection

1. What types of applications require a GUI?

_____

_____

2. Who is more likely to use a GUI, an end user or an administrator? Why?

_____

_____

3. The CLI program Xconfigurator is useful in fixing and reconfiguring X Window problems. At a terminal window, type in **man Xconfigurator** and read the online documentation.

Lab 10.1.3: CLI Interface

Estimated Time: 15 Minutes

Objective

In this lab, you navigate the Linux file system, and you learn how to use the navigation tools provided by Linux to locate files and folders. This lab covers the following commands:

- **cd**
- **ls**
- **pwd**
- **cal**
- **date**

Equipment

The following equipment is required for this exercise:

- Computer with Linux Red Hat 7.2 operating system installed

Scenario

You are setting up a new computer for a user. Before you can give this user the new computer, you need to create some directories and files that the user needs.

Procedure

Using this new computer that has the Linux operating system installed on it, you navigate through the file system and locate the user's home directory. You also use the file system to navigate through and check to make sure the necessary directories are in place.

Step 1: ls, pwd and cd Commands

1. Log in as the root user.

2. At the command line type the following:

```
ls
```

This displays the contents of the root's home directory. In the space below list the contents of this directory.

3. From within the root's home directory type the following:

```
cd ..
```

Press the **Enter** key. Make sure to include a space between the (cd and the ..). The **cd** .. command moves the user up one directory. The parent directory of the root's home directory is the root (/) of the Linux directory structure. The / and the /root directory only sound the same, they are two entirely different directories. The / is the highest level you can go in the Linux directory system. The /root is the home directory for the root user.

4. From the / type the following:

> `ls`

Press the **Enter** key. This displays the contents of the / directory. In the space below list the directories just below the root / (see Figure 10-13).

Figure 10-19   Root Directory Contents

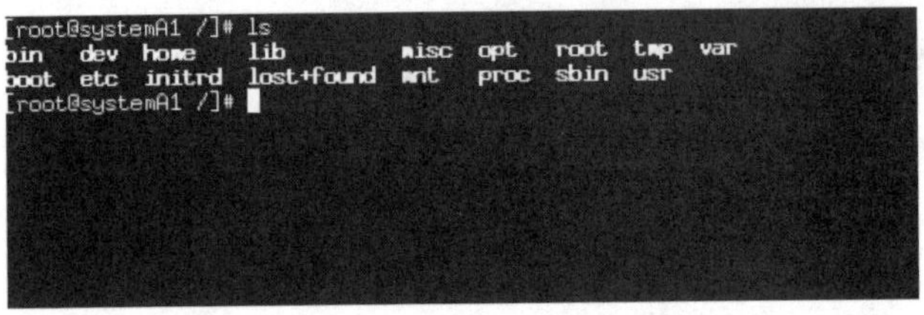

The contents of your / directory should look similar to the Figure 10-19.

5. From the root of the Linux directory structure type the following:

> `cd bin`

Press the **Enter** key. This changes the current active directory to the bin. Verify this with the **pwd** command. The **pwd** command prints the current working directory to the screen; type the following:

> `pwd`

Press the **Enter** key. In the space below, write down the output of the **pwd** command:

6. To list the contents of the /bin directory type the following:

> `ls`

Press the **Enter** key. Briefly describe the files/programs that are located in the /bin directory.

List three commonly used commands that can be found in the/bin directory.

Figure 10-20   Contents of the /bin directory

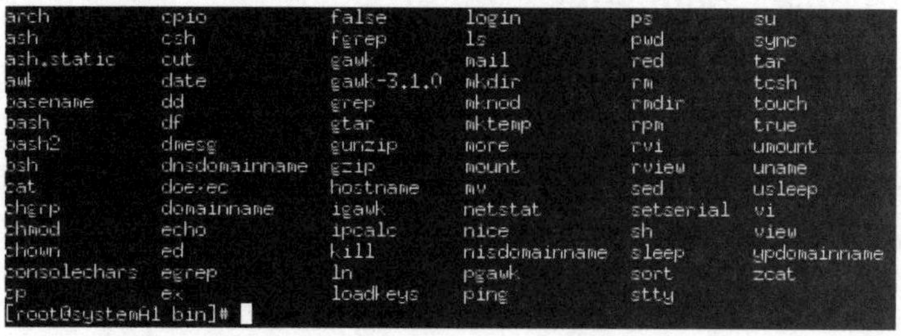

7. From the /bin directory, type the following command and press the **Enter** key:

    `cd`

When typed without switches, the **cd** command takes you to the user's home directory. Verify that you are in the /root home directory and type the following:

    `pwd`

Press the **Enter** key and write down the output of the **pwd** command.

8. From the /root home directory type the following and press the **Enter** key:

    `cd /etc`

This command takes you to the /etc directory. The / before the etc directory tells Linux to go up to the root (/) first and then down to the etc directory. From within the /root directory, you cannot simply type cd etc. Typing cd etc from within the /root directory tells Linux to look down first and the etc directory won't be found.

From within the /etc directory type the following:

    `ls`

Press the **Enter** key and briefly describe the contents of the /etc directory.

In the space below write the files that start with rc.

9. Return home by typing the following:

    `cd`

Press the **Enter** key and verify that you are in the home directory by typing the following:

    `pwd`

Write out the path:

Step 2: cal and date Commands

1. Use the **man** command and learn about the **cal** command; type the following:

```
man cal
```

Next, type the current month:

For example

```
cal 11 2002
```

Now try

```
cal 09 1752
```

Figure 10-21 shows a CLI calendar.

Figure 10-21   CLI Calendar

Linux did not get the month wrong. Do you know what happened to the 3rd through the 13th in September of 1752?

2. Use the **man** command and learn about the **date** command; type the following:

```
man date
```

Type

```
date
```

Then type

```
date -u
```

In the following space, describe the difference between the two outputs of **date** and that of **date –u**.

_____

_____

Reflection

Navigating the file system can be done with the X Windows GUI, similar to the way it is done in Windows. However, many experienced Linux users find it easier and faster to navigate using the CLI.

Lab 10.1.4: Linux Bash and C Shells

Estimated Time: 15 Minutes

Objective

In this lab, you use the following shells:

- bash
- csh
-

Equipment

The following equipment is required for this exercise:

- Computer with Linux Red Hat 7.2 installed and booted CLI window open

Scenario

Log in and access two Linux shells, the bash shell and the c shell. Initiate various commands to compare and contrast the two shells.

Procedures

Step 1: Shell Background Information

In your own words, answer the following questions:

1. What is a shell?

_____

_____

_____

2. Who wrote the bash and the c shells?

_____

_____

_____

Throughout this lab, you use the Linux **ps** command. The **ps** command gives a snapshot of the current processes (or jobs) that are running. Before starting this lab, learn more about the **ps** command by typing the following:

man ps

What are some significant switches that can be used with the **ps** command?

Note: All Linux shells have many common attributes. For example, the following keystrokes will perform the following functions:

Ctrl-C—Sends an interrupt signal to terminate a process

Ctrl-D—Sends an end of file to the running command

Ctrl-Z—Suspends the currently running program

Step 2: Shell Operations

If you are not already logged in, log in now with a student user account and password. Can you tell what shell you are in? Try typing in the following commands:

```
ps
```

and

```
echo $SHELL
```

The **echo** command replies back to the monitor (or echo) information about the current running shell (see Figure 10-22).

Figure 10-22 **echo $SHELL** *Command*

Does your screen look like this? What is the shell that is currently running?

Step 3: C Shell

1. Switch to the C shell. At the prompt type the following:

```
csh
```

What does the prompt look like? How is it different from the bash shell?

2. Run the **ps** command again by typing the following:

> `ps`

Describe the output of this command:

_____

Does your screen look similar to Figure 10-23?

Figure 10-23 csh shell Prompt

What is the Process Identification (PID) for the csh shell on your computer?

Step 4: Exit the C Shell

From the C shell, type the following:

`exit`

What shell did you end in?

_____

How do you know?

_____

Step 5: Exit the Bash Shell

From the bash shell, type the following:

`exit`

Where did you end up this time?

_____

Step 6: Shell Helpful Tips

If you are logged out in the previous step, log back in with a student account. Many useful keyboard combinations are part of the bash shell. For example, if you know a command starts with **<ca>** but you have forgotten the rest of the command, try typing the following:

ca+TAB *(without any spaces)*

What were the results? Now, go to the C shell (type **csh**) again and try the same command; type the following:

ca+TAB *(without any spaces)*

Did the same command work in the C shell? Explain why.

_____

_____

Go back to the bash shell when you are done and type the following:

`exit`

Step 7: Navigating the File Structure

Type the following:

`cd /`

This takes you to the / of the directory structure.

Next, from the root (/) of the bash shell, type the following:

`cd /h` *(then press the **Tab** key)*

Did it complete the command for you?

_____

Click the **Enter** key. What directory did you end up in?

_____

Try this same command sequence in the C shell. Does tab-competition work in the C shell?

_____

Reflection

Linux shells are generally not considered to be user-friendly. Between the bash shell and the C shell, which one do you consider to be easier—why?

_____

_____

_____

Worksheet 10.1.4: Linux Shells

1. The Linux shells operate as a _____.

True or False: _____ In Linux, the shell is integrated into the kernel and is always running.

Match the following items to the corresponding Linux Shell:

a. Korn Shell _____

b. C Shell _____

c. Bourne Again Shell _____

d. Bourne Shell _____

A. This shell was created as an enhanced extension of the Bourne Shell. This shell is referred to as the Bash Shell and is used for many UNIX-like systems, such as Linux.

B. This shell is not widely used because it is one of the more complicated shells to work with. It uses a much more complex syntax for shell programming than some other shells. For this reason, the C shell is not recommended for shell programming or for creating shell programs.

C. This is known as the original UNIX shell. The program name is (sh) and is known as the bash Shell in Linux systems. This shell provides all the (sh) functions and shell programming using shell script files.

D. This is a shell that combines the interactive features that make the C shell popular with the easier-to-use shell programming syntax of the Bourne Shell.

Lab 10.1.5: Using the Linux vi Editor

Estimated Time: 30-45 Minutes

Objective

In this lab, you perform the following tasks:

- Become familiar with the vi Editor
- Review the three vi modes
- Review keystrokes to move between vi modes
- Create a new file with vi Editor
- Invoke vi with show mode
- Review the save and quit commands
- Open an existing file with vi Editor
- Use editing commands
- Customize your session
- Use search commands

Equipment

The following equipment is required for this exercise:

- Login user ID (e.g. studentA1) and password assigned by your instructor
- Computer with Linux Red Hat 7.2 operating system installed

Scenario

In this lab, you use a UNIX text-editing tool: the vi (pronounced "vee eye") Editor. This text editor is primarily used for creating and modifying files that customize your work environment and for writing script files to automate tasks. System adminis-trators use text editors to create and modify system files used for networking, security, application sharing, and so on. The vi Editor became a part of the UNIX operating systems shortly after UNIX's inception and is universally available with UNIX systems including Linux. The vi Editor is a flexible and powerful editor with many options. These options are reviewed here with examples of their use.

For users learning to become system administrators, it is important to know how to use vi Editor. It is sometimes the only full screen editor available to edit crucial system files. Examples of these include scripts and environment control files.

Skill in using vi Editor is also needed if the windowing system is not available. The vi Editor is a useful tool when working remotely on other Linux workstations or servers. Administrators routinely login remotely or telnet to another Linux computer to perform maintenance and troubleshooting tasks using the vi Editor. The availability and operation of vi Editor is consistent across all UNIX/Linux platforms.

Use the diagram of the sample Class File System directory tree to assist with this lab.

Step 1: Logging In to Linux and Going into X-Window (startx)

Log in with the username and password assigned to you by your instructor in the KDE entry box.

Step 2: Accessing the Command Line

Select **Terminal** from the task bar to open a terminal window.

Step 3: Reviewing the Three vi Modes

There are three modes of operation in vi Editor. Understanding the function of these three modes is the key to working with vi Editor. All commands available with vi Editor can be classified in one of the three modes. The following table lists the modes and a brief description of each. Review the three modes and answer the following questions:

Mode	Function / Characteristics
Command mode	Initial default mode for creating and editing files, cursor positioning and modification of existing text. All commands are initiated from this mode.
Insert mode	Used for entry of new text. Entering an insert command such as i (insert), a (append), and o (open new line) will take you from command mode to entry mode. Entry commands are stand-alone and are entered without pressing the Enter key.
Last-line mode	Used for saving your work and quitting vi Editor. Type a colon (:) to get to this mode. Pressing the **Enter** key or **Esc** key returns to command mode.

1. Which vi mode is primarily used to enter new text?

_____

2. Which vi mode is used to save your work and quit vi Editor?

_____

3. When you start the vi Editor, which mode is the default?

_____

Step 4: Reviewing Keystrokes to Move Between vi Modes

The following table shows how to switch modes and get from one mode to another. Review the keystrokes required to move between modes and answer the following questions.

From Mode	To Mode	Commands / Keystrokes
Command	Entry	i (input), o (open new line), a (append to existing line)
Entry	Command	Press **Esc** (Escape)
Command	Last-line	Colon (:)
Last-line	Command	Press **Esc** or **Enter**
Entry	Last-line	Press **Esc** to return to Command mode, then enter a colon
Last-line	Entry	Press **Enter** or **Esc** to return to Command mode, then enter an insert command

1. Which single-character alphabetic commands puts vi in Entry mode?

_____

2. Which key returns vi to Command mode from either Last-line or Entry mode?

_____

3. Which command puts vi into Last-line mode from Command mode?

_____

Step 5: Creating a New File with vi Editor

The vi Editor is started from the command line. Whenever you invoke vi Editor, you are opening a file. You can specify the name of the file you want to create or edit when you start vi Editor, or you can open a new file to be named later. It is common to start vi Editor and specify a filename. If the file exists, it is opened for editing. If the file does not exist, it is created.

Command Format: **vi [option(s)] [filename]**

1. If you are logged in as the root user, switch users to another account (**su -**). If you don't know of another account, ask your instructor for an available account. Verify that you are in the home directory. What command did you use?

2. Open a new file called myvifile using the command **vi myvifile**. What does the vi document screen look like?

3. Press the lowercase letter **i** to begin inserting text at the first line. Is there any indication on the screen that you are in Insert Entry mode?

4. Type your name. If you make a mistake, do not try to correct it at this time. Were you able to enter text in Insert mode?

5. Press the **Esc** key to leave Insert Entry mode and return to Command mode. Is there any indication on the screen that you are back in Command mode?

6. Type a colon (**:**) to go from Command mode to Last-line mode. Are you now at the bottom-left corner of the screen at a colon (:) prompt? If not, press **Esc** again and enter another colon.

7. Type a lowercase **w** (write–[—]to save your new file), followed by a lowercase **q** (quit—to exit the vi Editor), and press **Enter**. What was the result of the **wq** commands? Are you back to the command prompt now?

8. The new file should be saved in your practice directory on the hard disk. Display a long listing of this directory to verify that your file is there (**ls –l**). How many bytes are in the file?

Step 6: Reviewing the Save and Quit Commands

In the previous steps, you created a file and saved it with the **w** (write) command and exited vi Editor with the **q** (quit) command. There are several save and quit commands available with vi Editor. The following table lists some of the more common ones.

Note: Save and quit commands (except for ZZ) are entered only when in Last-line mode.

Save and Quit Commands

Command	Meaning
:w	Write buffer (Save changes and continue working in vi Editor)
:w new_filename	Write buffer to new_filename (continue working in vi)
:wq	Write buffer (save changes) and quit vi
ZZ (upper case)	Save changes and quit vi. Alternative to :wq
:q!	Quit without saving changes
:wq!	Write buffer (save changes) and quit vi (The ! will override Read only permissions if you are the owner of the file.)

1. Most save and quit commands are entered in which mode?

2. Which command allows you to exit vi Editor and not save any of your changes?

3. Which two commands listed in the table perform the same function?

4. Which command allows you to save the current file you are editing under another name and remain in vi Editor to continue editing the current file?

Step 7: Opening an Existing File

If you start vi Editor and specify an existing filename, it is opened for editing. Here, you can add some new text in Entry mode and try a few cursor positioning commands.

1. Open myvifile, which you created earlier using the command **vi myvifile**. What does the vi document screen look like?

2. Position the cursor at the end of your name and press the lowercase letter **a** to append to the line you typed earlier. Type some text, and then press **Enter** for a hard return. Then type some more text. Enter about three lines of text this way. What mode are you currently in?

3. Press the **Esc** key to leave Insert mode and return to Command mode. In Command mode, can you position your cursor (with the arrow keys) for additional editing?

4. You can move your cursor with the arrow keys while in the various entry modes and you will remain in that mode. The following table contains some of the more common cursor positioning keys and commands. If you use the alphabetic commands while in an entry mode, they will be entered as text. You need to press **Esc** to get to Command mode to use them. Practice using these while you are editing this file. Which character moves you back one word at a time?

Step 8: Cursor Positioning Commands

Command	Meaning
j or Down arrow	Move down one line
k or Up arrow	Move up one line
Space bar	Move right (forward) one character
w	Move forward one word (including punctuation)
Back Space	Move left one character (check for accuracy)
B	Move back one word (including punctuation)
$	Move to end of line
0 (zero) or ^	Move to beginning of line
Return	Move down to beginning of next line

1. Press the up arrow to position the cursor until it is on line two. Use the **j** (jump down) command to move down and then use the **k** (kick up) command to move back to line two.

2. Type a lowercase **o** to open a new line below the line your cursor is on and enter some new text. What mode are you in now?

3. Press the **Esc** key again to leave Open line Entry mode and return to Command mode.

4. Type a colon (:) to go to Last-line mode; then save and quit this file when you are finished. If this were a real file and you had made some mistakes and did not want to save the changes you made, what Last-line mode command would you use?

5. The new file should be saved in your practice directory on the hard disk. Display a long listing of this directory to verify that your file is there. How many bytes is the file?

Step 9: Copying and Pasting Text

Many editing commands can be used to modify existing text in a file. These include commands for deleting and changing text. The majority of these commands are entered while in command mode.

1. Open a new document with vi Editor. What did you name the file?

2. Insert some text – Add five or more lines of text and press **Enter** at the end of each line. Make some mistakes as you type.

Delete some text. To delete text while in command mode, position the cursor to the desired location and use the options shown in the following table to delete your mistakes.

Note: These commands are all lowercase and are entered without the Enter key.

Basic Text Deletion Commands

Command	Meaning
x	Delete character at the cursor
dw	Delete word (or part of word to right of cursor)
3dw	Delete three words
dd	Delete line containing the cursor
3dd	Delete three lines

1. Undo and change some text. To change text and undo changes, use the commands shown in the next table. *Note*: Many of these commands change you to Insert mode until you press Escape.

Note: These commands are all lowercase.

Undo and Change Commands

Command	Meaning
cw	Change word (or part of word) at the cursor location to the end of the word
3cw	Change three words
r	Replace character at cursor with one other character
u	Undo previous command

1. Copy and paste text by using the following options:

Copy and Paste Some Text

Command	Meaning
yy	Yank a copy of a line and place in the clipboard
p	Put (paste) yanked or deleted line below current line
P (upper case)	Put (paste) yanked or deleted line above current line

1. Save the file and quit vi Editor.

What command did you use?

_____

Step 10: Customizing Your Session

The vi Editor includes options for customizing your edit sessions. These options are summarized in the next table. The **set** command is used from Last-line mode to control these options. The **set nu** option shows line numbers and is used frequently when writing programs and script files. The line numbers are not part of the file.

1. Open the document you just created with vi Editor. Use the commands in the table to customize your vi session.

Session Customizing Commands

Command	Meaning
:set nu	Show line numbers
:set nonu	Hide line numbers
:set showmode	Display current mode of operation
:set noshowmode	Turn off mode display
:set	Display all vi variables set
:set all	Display all possible vi variables and their current settings

Step 11: Using Search Commands

The commands in the following table allow you to perform advanced editing, such as finding lines or conducting searches for text. The forward slash (/) and the question mark (?) search options are also Last-line commands, but they do not require a colon first. The next (n) and next previous (N) commands can find the next occurrence after the /string or ?string commands found what you were looking for.

Basic Search Commands

Command	Meaning
G (upper case)	Go to last line of file
:21	Go to line 21
/string	Search forward for string
?string	Search backward for string
n	Find next occurrence of string

Use the commands in the table to practice searching for a particular line or string of text.

Quit vi Editor without saving any changes. What command did you use?

Step 12: Closing the Terminal Window and Logging Out

Double-click the dash button in the upper-left corner of the screen, and click the **EXIT** icon on the front panel.

Worksheet 10.1.5: vi Editor

1. Linux includes a powerful editing tool call the _____ that allows editing of the configuration and script files and the creation of some configuration and script files.

2. You can access Edit mode by choosing the command _____.

3. There are three modes of operation in vi:

   a.

   _____

   _____

   b.

   _____

   _____

   c.

   _____

   _____

4. Fill in this chart:

Mode	Functions / Characteristics
Command Mode	
Entry Mode	
Last-Line Mode	

5. Describe the difference between vi Editor and another text editor such as Microsoft's notepad.

   _____

   _____

   _____

   _____

   _____

Lab 10.2.1: Adding Users in Linux

Estimated Time: 20 Minutes

Objective

In this lab, you learn how to create user accounts by using the Linux Red Hat 7.x operating system.

Equipment

The following equipment is required for this exercise:

- Computer with Linux installed
- The computer will boot to the CLI not the GUI (not to X Windows at startup)
-

Scenario

The XYZ Company installed a server running Linux. The company asked you to log onto the server and create users.

Procedures

Until now, each workstation acted independently from other computers. Each student will create user accounts and these accounts will be used in later labs.

To complete the following steps, each student needs to be at the command line. If X Window was launched at bootup, students need to open a terminal window.

Step 1: Account Planning

From the drawing in Figure 10-24, plan out how many accounts need to be added.

Figure 10-24   Classroom Layout

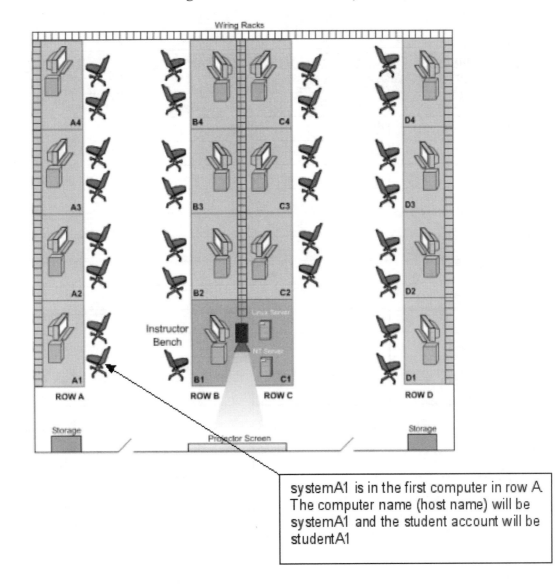

systemA1 is in the first computer in row A.
The computer name (host name) will be
systemA1 and the student account will be
studentA1

Assign each computer a name, which will also identify its location. User accounts can be added to the system name to identify not only the computer but also the user at that location.

For example, students use systemA1; therefore, a user account with the name studentA1 will be used.

Assign a password that is the same as the computer name to make the initial login easier.

In the following space, write out a user account list. Include the computer you are working on.

Computer Name/Location	User Account/Name	Password	Comments

Example of user accounts and host names:

Computer Name/Location	User Account/Name	Password	Comments
A1	studentA1	studentA1	
A2	studentA2	studentA2	
A3	studentA3	studentA3	
A4	studentA4	studentA4	
B1	instructorB1	instructorB1	Instructor, Windows Computer
B2	studentB2	studentB2	
B3	studentB3	studentB3	
B4	studentB4	studentB4	
C1	instructorC1	instructorC1	Instructor, Linux Computer
C2	studentC2	studentC2	
C3	studentC3	studentC3	
C4	studentC4	studentC4	
D1	studentD1	studentD1	
D2	studentD2	studentD2	
D3	studentD3	studentD3	
D4	studentD4	studentD4	

Step 2: useradd Command

At the command prompt, type the following command:

```
man useradd
```

What do the following switches do?

-c

_____

-d

_____

-e

_____

Does the **useradd** command create a home directory for the user by default, and if so where?

_____

Step 3: passwd Command

The **useradd** command by itself does not automatically allow a user to log in. A password must first be assigned to the user account. This is done with the **passwd** command.

At the command prompt, type the following command:

```
man passwd
```

Briefly describe the following passwd switches:

-k

_____

-l

_____

-u

_____

-d

_____

What other means of password protection does the **man passwd** page discuss?

_____

Step 4: Adding Users

For this step, make sure that you are logged in as the root user. If you are not already root, use the **su – root** command with the root's password.

With the list from Step 1, create accounts for all other users in the lab.

Look at the example in Figure 10-25.

Figure 10-25 Creating a User Account

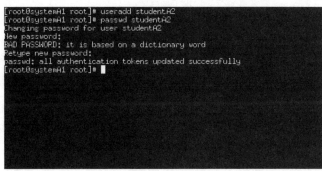

Note: Part of the password for these accounts can be found in a dictionary, (the word "student"). Linux warns against using these passwords for security reasons but it will accept them. All passwords must be entered twice.

Notice the previous example; this is a two-step process. First, create the account with the **useradd** command and then give the new user account a password with the **passwd** command.

1. Type the following:

    useradd student*XX*

    (where *XX* is the username from the table in Step 1), and press **Enter**.

2. Type the following:

    passwd student*XX*

    Use the student account for the password. Linux asks you to enter the password twice to check for accuracy.

3. Continue this procedure until all the users are added to the systems.

Step 5: Account Verification

In this step, verify that the accounts were created correctly in Step 4 by using the **finger** command.

To learn about the **finger** command, type the following:

    man finger

Experiment with the **finger** command; type the following:

    finger root

Briefly describe the output of this command:

_____

_____

Verify that the accounts were created correctly in Step 4. Randomly pick six accounts and use the **finger** command to see if they were created correctly.

List your results in the following table.

Account name	Verified Y/N

Step 6: Deleting Users

To delete an account, the Linux administrator uses the **userdel** command. Read the man page on the **userdel** command; type the following:

        `man userdel`

Describe the –**r** switch when it is run with the **userdel** command:

_____

To test the **userdel** command create a temporary account; type the following:

        `useradd temp123`

(*Note*: This account does not need a password because this is only a temporary account.)

To see if the account was created, type the following:

        `finger temp123`

Was a home directory created? Y/N

Next, delete the temp account; type the following:

`userdel -r temp123`

Does the account still exist?

Type the following:

```
finger temp123
```

What was the output of this command?

_____

Troubleshooting

To create accounts in Linux, you must be logged onto the server as an Administrator. If you encounter problems while creating these accounts, verify that you have the necessary administrative privileges by logging off of the server and logging on again using the Administrator account.

Reflection

Why is it important that only an administrator is allowed to create user accounts?

_____
_____
_____
_____

Lab 10.2.3: Creating Groups in Linux

Estimated Time: 30 Minutes

Objective

In this lab, you learn how to create, rename, and delete groups using the Linux operating system, and then add members to that group.

Equipment

The following equipment is required for this exercise:

- Computer system with Linux Red Hat 7.2 operating system installed

Scenario

You have learned that a few members in the engineering department, who are using Linux, are going to be working on classified documents. They need to have their own group created, so they can keep these documents in certain folders that only their group will have permissions to. You have been asked to create a group and add the members to this group.

Procedures

In this lab, you first create the engineering group and then add the localuser1 user account to this group. You then rename the group and delete the group.

Tips Before You Begin, Remember:

- User permissions apply to the owner of the file or directory.
- Group permissions apply to the members of the group that are assigned to a file or directory..
- Linux stores group information in the /etc/group file.

Step 1: Creating a Group and Adding Users to the Group

Note: The account studentA5 is used throughout this lab as an example. Ask your instructor for the appropriate account for your particular lab situation.

1. Log in with the root account.

2. At the command prompt, type the following:

   ```
   groupadd Engineering
   ```

   Press **Enter**; this creates the Engineering group.

3. Next, add a student account to the new Engineering group; type the following:

   ```
   usermod -G Engineering studentA5
   ```

   Press **Enter**, this adds the studentA5 account to the engineering group.

4. Verify that the new group has been created; type the following:

   ```
   grep studentA5 /etc/group
   ```

   The **grep** command looks for strings of text. In this case, we asked the **grep** command to look in the /etc/group file for anything named studentA5. What were your results?

   _____

   _____

   Does your output look similar to the example in Figure 10-26?

Figure 10-26 **grep** *Command*

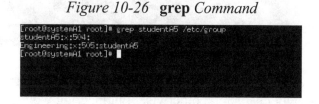

Step 2: Creating a Working Folder for the Engineering Group

1. As the root user, go to the /home directory; type the following:

   ```
   cd /home
   ```

2. Create a new directory; type the following:

   ```
   mkdir Eng
   ```

3. Verify that the new dir exists; type the following:

```
ls -l
```

4. Change the ownership of the Eng directory with the following command:

```
chgrp Engineering Eng
```

5. Verify that ownership has changed from the root to Engineering: type the following:

```
ls -l
```

Who is now the owner of the Engineering directory?

6. Change the permissions of the Engineering directory; type the following:

```
chmod 771 Eng
```

7. Verify directory permissions; type the following:

```
ls -l
```

Write down the permissions. Do they look like the example in Figure 10-27?

_____

_____

_____

Figure 10-27 **ls –l** *Command*

Note: The owner of the Eng directory is the root user. The group is Engineer. Linux can display only eight characters; otherwise, Engineering would appear. Both the root account and the Engineering group have the same Read, Write, and eXecute permissions. In the last group, everyone has eXecute privileges only.

Step 3: Creating Files in the Eng Directory

1. Switch users from root to the studentA5 account; type the following:

```
su - studentA5
```

2. Go into the Eng directory; type the following:

```
cd /home/Eng
```

3. Create a file; type the following:

```
touch grp_file
```

4. Verify that the new file was created; type the following:

```
ls -l
```

Is the file grp_file there? Y/N

5. Now switch the user, who is not a member of the Engineering group, to a studentA1 account; type the following:

```
su - studentA1
```

6. Go to the /home/Eng directory; type the following:

```
cd /home/Eng
```

7. Create a file; type the following:

```
touch grp_file1
```

What happened?

Try typing the following:

```
ls -al
```

What happened? Do you know why?

Step 4: Deleting the Eng Directory

1. Log back in as the root user; type the following:

```
su - root
```

Enter the password and press **Enter**.

2. Verify that you are the root user; type the following:

```
whoami
```

3. Go to the /home directory; type the following:

```
cd/ home
```

4. Delete the Eng dir and its contents; type the following:

```
rm -r Eng
```

When prompted to delete the files and the directory, type **Y** for yes.

5. Verify that the Eng directory has been removed; type the following:

```
ls -l
```

Is the Eng directory gone? Y/N

Step 5: Renaming a Group

1. At the command prompt, type the following:

```
groupmod -n Engineers Engineering
```

2. Verify that the group name changed; type the following:

```
grep Engineers/etc/group
```

Press **Enter**. This renames the group.

Step 6: Deleting a Group

1. At the command prompt, type the following:

```
groupdel Engineers
```

Press **Enter**. This deletes the group.

2. Verify with the **grep** command; type the following:

grep Engineers/etc/group

Troubleshooting

To create accounts in Linux, you must be logged onto the server as the root user. If you encounter problems while creating these accounts, verify that you have the necessary administrative privileges by logging off of the server and logging on again using the root account.

Reflection

Why is it important that only an administrator be allowed to create groups?

_____

_____

_____

_____

Lab 10.3.1: Creating Directories in Linux

Estimated Time: 15 Minutes

Objective

In this lab, you learn how to create files and directories with the Linux operating system.

Equipment

The following equipment is required for this exercise:

- Computer system with Linux Red Hat 7.2 operating system installed
-

Scenario

The IT department in your company purchased some new computer systems. You are asked to create some new directories and files on the server for the people that are going to be receiving these new computers.

Procedures

In the first step of this lab, you create a directory or folder. Then, in the second step of the lab, you create a file and save it inside the directory.

Step 1: Logging In

Log in using a student account for this lab.

For example, at the terminal window, type the following:

```
studentA1
```

Then, type the password for student A1.

Step 2: The mkdir Command

The **mkdir** command creates directories and subdirectories. Run the following command:

```
man mkdir
```

What does the **–p** switch do when it is run in conjunction with the **mkdir** command?

Step 3: Creating Directories

1. The following command sequence will not work unless you are in your own home directory; type the following:

```
cd
```

Verify that you are in your home directory by using the **pwd** command. Next, create the directory structure by typing in the following command as in Figure 10-28:

```
mkdir -p chemistry/experiments/week3
```

Figure 10-28   Creating the Directory Structure

Verify that the directories were created correctly; type the following:

```
ls -R
```

Be sure to use a capital R with the **ls** command. Describe the results.

Your results should look similar to the screen in Figure 10-29.

*Figure 10-29   **ls –R** Command Output*

2. Next, create another directory in the chemistry directory; type the following:

    `cd chemistry`

    This changes the current working directory to the chemistry directory. From the chemistry directory, type the following:

    `mkdir laboratory`

    Verify that the laboratory directory was created; type the following:

    `ls`

    Is the subdirectory called laboratory there?

    Y/N

    Are there now two directories in the chemistry directory?

    Y/N

3. In the space below draw a picture of your home directory. Create a graphical representation of your home directory including all the new directories that were created in the steps in this lab.

Reflection

If you did not use the **–p** switch with the **mkdir** command, how would you have created the preceding directory structure?

Lab 10.3.5: Managing Run Levels

Estimated Time: 20 Minutes

Objective

In this lab, you learn the concepts and purposes of the run levels in a Linux environment.

Equipment

The following equipment is required for this exercise:

- Computer with Linux Red Hat 7.X installed

Scenario

You are the system administrator of a large company. You have a group of Linux servers whose resources need to be given to the incoming user requests. You want the systems to boot up automatically into text mode instead of GUI mode. The systems resources can be used for other things than running the X Window GUI. To accomplish this, you decide to permanently change the default run level.

Procedures

Step 1: Manually Changing the Run Level

Note: Log in as the root user prior to starting this lab.

First, make sure that your system is booted up correctly and that the X Window GUI is running.

1. Open a terminal window and type the following command at the command prompt:

```
init 3 or /sbin/init 3
```

Your system should exit the GUI mode and take a few seconds to terminate some running processes; then, you will enter text mode.

2. After the login prompt appears, log back in as the root user.

3. After you successfully logged in, type the following command at the shell prompt:

```
init 5 or /sbin/init 5
```

The GUI login interface now loads and you need to log in to the X Window session. Log in again with the root account. At this point, you have successfully learned how to manually change the run level.

Step 2: Permanently Changing the Run Level

1. Open a terminal window. Navigate to and open the **/etc/inittab** file with the vi Editor. To do this, enter the following command at the shell prompt:

```
vi /etc/inittab
```

It might be a good idea to read over this file because there is a lot of useful information here regarding your system's configuration. To change the default run level on a Linux system permanently is a simple process involving editing the /etc/inittab file—specifically, the id:5:initdefault: line. This line indicates a system that is set to run level five by default.

2. As stated in the scenario, you want to change the default run level manually so that the system automatically starts in text mode instead of GUI mode. To do this, change the **id:5:initdefault:** line to the following:

```
id:3:initdefault:
```

3. Now, you want to save this edit. To do this, you need to press the **Esc** key on the keyboard; then, type **:wq** and press **Enter**. This should return you to a shell prompt.

4. Remember that you still might have other labs to do after this one, so you might want to change the default run level back to run level 5. To do this, repeat Steps 1 through 3 and change the run level back to 5 instead of 3.

Reflection

Are there any other purposes that you can see where permanently changing the default run level might be an advantage? Is it possible to have certain programs start at different run levels?

Lab 10.4.2: HTTP Apache Web Server

Estimated Time: 55 Minutes

Objective

In this lab, you learn to install the Apache web server. You examine the configuration files, check the status of the HTTPD daemon, and test the Apache server using Netscape.

Equipment

The following equipment is required for this exercise:

- Computer running Linux Red Hat 7.2 or greater
- CD-ROM with the Apache RPM

Scenario

You are the administrator of a Linux server. You need to install the Apache web application and test all of its configuration files.

Procedures

Log in as the root user and install the Apache web server. Check the Apache configuration files and the HTTPD daemon. Launch a local web page and test it both locally and on other classroom computers.

Step 1: Mounting the Apache RPM CD-ROM

1. Boot the Linux computer and log in as the root user. Launch X Window (use the **startx** command) and make sure that you are using the KDE desktop (see Figure 10-30).

Figure 10-30 **startx** *Command*

Open the Home Directory (the Linux equivalent of Windows Explorer) by clicking (once) on the folder in the taskbar.

Go to the desktop and look for the CD-ROM icon. In some Linux systems, the CD-ROM can be mounted automatically. Click the CD-ROM to view the contents. If you cannot see the contents of the CD-ROM, you might need to run the following CLI command from a terminal window. Again, you must be logged in with the root account for this command to work; type the following:

```
mount /mnt/cdrom
```

Go to the KDE Home Directory window and click the CD-ROM icon. The contents of the CD-ROM will now be visible in KDE.

Step 2: Installing the Apache RPM

1. When the CD-ROM is open, go to the following directory to see the contents in
Figure 10-31:

```
/RedHat/RPMS
```

Figure 10-31   Red Hat Packages

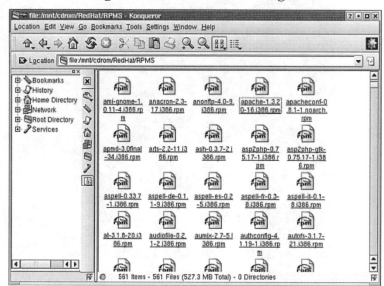

Note: If you do not find the Apache RPM, it might be located on the second disk that
came with Red Hat.

2. Click the **Install** button. This installs Apache(see Figure 10-32).

Figure 10-32   Kpackage

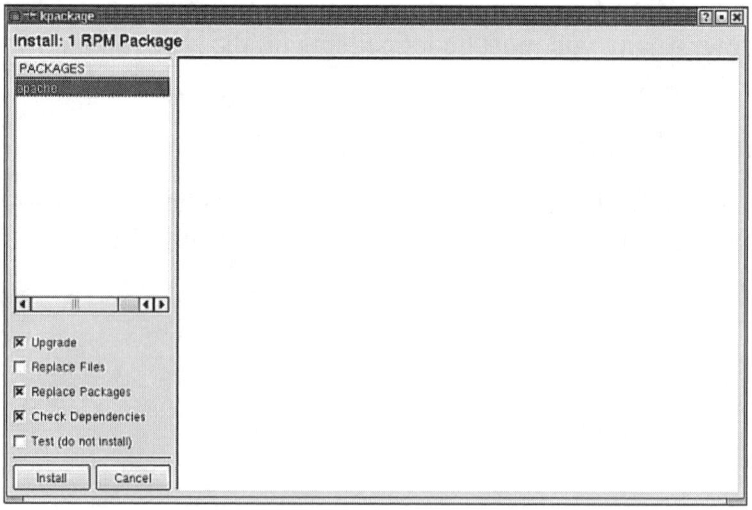

To verify that the Apache server installed correctly, run the following command from the terminal window; type the following:

```
rpm -q apache
```

3. Write down the results. If Apache installed correctly, your screen should look like Figure 10-33.

Figure 10-33 **rpm –q** *Command*

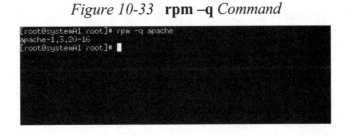

4. After Apache has been installed, remove the CD-ROM. To do this, go back to the KDE Home Directory and locate the CD-ROM. Again, the CD-ROM icon is usually located under the desktop directory. After it is located, right-click the CD-ROM and select the eject option.

The CD-ROM can also be ejected using a command from the CLI. To unmount the CD-ROM, from a terminal window; type the following:

```
umount/mnt/cdrom
```

Now press the eject button on the CD-ROM itself and the CD-ROM will come out.

Step 3: Checking the Apache Installation Files

1. It is important for the Linux administrator to know where the RPM has placed the Apache configuration files and directories. Next is a list of the import Apache files and directories with a brief description of each:

Use the **cd** command (from a terminal window) and go to the following directory; type the following:

```
cd /etc/httpd/conf
```

2. The /etc/httpd/conf directory is where the configuration file for Apache is located. Use the **ls** command to verify that the file exists:

```
ls -a
```

Is there a file called **httpd.conf** present in this directory?

Yes/No

3. Go to the following directory, ; type the following:

```
cd /var/www/html/
```

> This directory is where Apache finds the html startup page. Use the **ls** command to verify that the file exists, type:

```
ls -a
```

> Is there a file called index.html present in this directory? Yes/No

4. Go to the following directory; use the **cd** command:

```
cd /etc/init.d/
```

> This directory contains the HTTPD daemon. A daemon is a small application that runs as a background task. The HTTPD daemon must be running for the Apache web server to work.

> Using the **ls** command, is there a file in this directory called httpd? Yes/No

Step 4: Apache config File

1. To become familiar with the Apache config file, run the following command from the command line; type

```
more /etc/httpd/conf/httpd.conf
```

> This is a long file; just skim it and do not make any changes. The # before most of the lines signifies a comment. Reading the comments is one of the best ways to understand how the Apache web server works.

2. Can you tell from the httpd configuration file what TCP port number Apache uses?

> *Note*: To exit the more command and return to the terminal window, type the letter **q**.

Step 5: Apache Home Page

1. The Apache index.html (Apache's startup page) file runs the following command:

```
vi/var/www/html/index.html
```

> This file contains the startup page text. Change the name of the startup page by editing this file. Change the main heading of this page to your student login name or any name your instructor gives you in place of the highlighted text.

```
<!DOCTYPE HTML PUBLIC "-//W3C//DTD HTML 3.2 Final//EN">

<HTML>

 <HEAD>

  <TITLE>Test Page for the Apache Web Server on Red Hat Linux</TITLE>

 </HEAD>

<!-- Background white, links blue (unvisited), navy (visited), red (active) -->

<BODY BGCOLOR="#FFFFFF">


  <H1 ALIGN="CENTER">studentA1</H1>

  This page is used to test the proper operation of the Apache Web server after

  it has been installed.  If you can read this page, it means that the Apache

  Web server installed at this site is working properly.


  <HR WIDTH="50%">


  <H2 ALIGN="CENTER">If you are the administrator of this website:</H2>

  <P>

  You may now add content to this directory, and replace this page.  Note that

  until you do so, people visiting your website will see this page, and not your

  content.

  </P>
```

Exit the vi Editor and be sure to save; type the following

:wq

Step 6: HTTPD Daemon Status

1. Next, verify the HTTPD daemon status by typing in the following command:

/etc/init.d/httpd status

What is the status of the HTTPD daemon? Write down the results:

The following is an example of an HTTPD daemon that has been stopped:

```
[root@systemA1 root]# /etc/rc.d/init.d/httpd status
httpd is stopped
[root@systemA1 root]#
```

If the HTTPD daemon is stopped, enter the following command:

/etc/init.d/httpd start

Write down the results:

Note: To stop Apache, type the following:

 /etc/init.d/httpd httpd stop

Step 7: Looking at the Home Page in Netscape

1. Go back to the KDE desktop and launch the Netscape browser. Netscape will be under the K button. Go to the Internet subdirectory.

2. After Netscape has loaded, go to the following URL:

   http://localhost

   You see your local Apache server index.html file (see Figure 10-34).

   Did you see your student name at the top of the page? Yes/No

Figure 10-34   Apache Web Browser Access

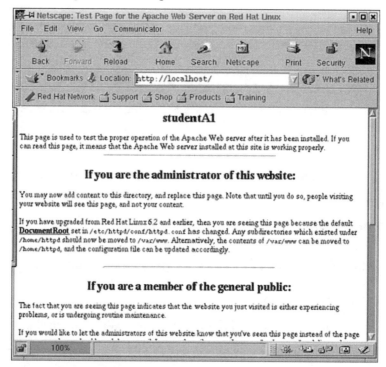

Step 8: Connecting to Your Neighbors

From a terminal window run the following command:

```
ifconfig
```

Find the IP address of the eth0. Write down the IP address and give it to other students in the class. Have them type in your IP address in their Netscape browser.

Example: http://192.168.5.5

Can they see your web page? Can you see their web page?

Troubleshooting

Did the web page work? If not, go through this checklist:

- Is Apache installed correctly? Use the **rpm –q apache** command.

- Were the configuration files in the correct directories?

- Is the HTTPD daemon running? Test it: **/etc/init.d/httpd status**

- Did the Web server work locally but your neighbors could not see it?

- Check the network connections. Make sure you are not behind a firewall.

Reflection

With a web server up and running, your Linux system now needs to be more reliable than ever. In the following space, identify five hardware/software issues that affect a computer's reliability. After each item, list what you could do as the Linux adminis-trator to make your computer more reliable.

_____

_____

_____

_____

_____

_____

Lab 10.4.3: Configuring FTP Services in Linux

Estimated Time: 25 Minutes

Objective

In this lab, you configure a Linux Red Hat 7.2 computer with FTP services and create a FTP server.

Equipment

For this exercise, you need a computer system with Linux Red Hat 7.2 (or greater) installed.

Scenario

The Marketing Director of the XYZ Company asked you to create an FTP site so that employees in the marketing and sales department can access and download files when away from the office. It is your job to create an FTP site on the server for them to access.

Procedures

In Linux Red Hat 7.2, the FTP services are not started by default. In this lab, you need to navigate to the configuration file first to start the FTP services. In the first step of this lab, you configure the FTP configuration file. In the second step of this lab, you start the FTP services and build the content that will be on the FTP server. The procedures for starting the FTP services will be done in much the same way that the Telnet services are started.

Step 1: Configuring the FTP Server

1. Log in with the root account. FTP services can be started only with the root account. You also want to make sure that you are at the CLI command prompt. If you are in the GUI interface, open a terminal emulator window.

2. After you are at the command prompt interface, type the following:

```
cd/etc/xinetd.d
```

This changes you to the proper directory where the Telnet configuration file is located.

3. Next, type the following:

```
ls
```

This displays a list of all the configuration files in the xinetd.d directory.

4. Locate the wu-ftpd configuration file. Is the wu-ftpd file in this directory?

> If you do not find the wu-ftp file, you need to install it now. Ask your instructor or lab aide for help.

5. At the command prompt, type the following:

```
vi wu-ftpd
```

> This allows you to use the vi Editor to change the Telnet configuration file.

6. After the vi Editor window opens, press **i** on the keyboard to enter Insert mode. Locate the "disable = yes" line in the configuration file, as shown in Figure 10-35.

Figure 10-35   Configuring FTP Access

7. Use your arrow keys on the keyboard to move the cursor to delete the word "yes" and replace it with "no." This changes the configuration file to allow FTP access to your server.

8. To exit the vi Editor, press **Esc**, then press the **:** key, and then type **wq**. This saves the changes that you made.

Step 2: xinetd Daemon

> Before testing the FTP services, you need to make sure that the FTP daemon is running. The daemon that runs the FTP services is called xinetd.

1. From the command prompt, type the following:

```
/etc/rc.d/init.d/xinetd stop
```

2. Next, start the xinetd daemon; type the following:

```
/etc/rc.d/init.d/xinetd start
```

3. Check the status of the xinetd daemon; type the following:

```
/etc/rc.d/init.d/xinetd status
```

In the following space write down the status of the xinetd daemon?

_____

_____

Figure 10-36 demonstrates the xinetd daemon being stopped and started.

Figure 10-36   Restarting the xinetd Daemon

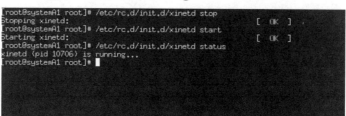

Step 3: Testing the FTP Properties

1. To test if your FTP services are working properly from a terminal window, type the following:

       ftp localhost

   This command uses your system to access the Telnet services on your system.

2. The Linux system attempts to make a Telnet connection to your system through the local loopback address 127.0.0.1. It runs through the login procedure and prompts you to enter a username and password.

3. Log in using a student account; do not use the root account to log on. When prompted, type the student account name and password.

4. If you get a connection to the system, you have successfully configured your Linux Red Hat Server for FTP access.

Figure 10-37 demonstrates a successful FTP Login

Figure 10-37   Successful FTP Login

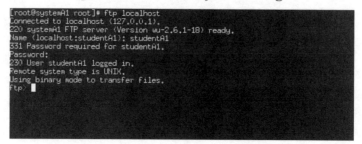

5. To see the current working directory, type the following:

```
pwd
```

6. To see the files in the current directory, type the following:

```
ls -a
```

7. To exit the FTP session, type the following:

```
bye
```

Step 4: Connecting to Other FTP Systems (Optional)

To complete this exercise, you need to work with another student on a system that is networked to yours.

1. From a terminal window, type the following:

```
ifconfig
```

Write down the IP address of eth0. Exchange IP addresses with a classmate.

2. Create a temporary user for the FTP purposes; type the following:

```
adduser ftpclient
```

3. Give the new ftpclient a password; type the following:

```
passwd ftpclient
```

When prompted, make the password the same as the account name, which is **ftp client.**

4. Create a file that can be viewed and transferred. First, go into the newly created ftpclient home directory, and type the following:

```
cd/home/ftpclient
```

Next, type the following:

```
touch hostname
```

The name of the file that you create with the **touch** command will be the same as your computer's host name. As an example, if the host name is systemA1, the command to create the file would be **touch systemA1**. Verify that this file exists with the **ls** command.

5. FTP to your classmate's computer. With the IP address from Step 1, type the following:

```
ftp IPaddress
```

Log in using the ftpclient account and password.

6. After you logged in to your classmate's computer, FTP their file to your computer; type the following:

```
get hostname
```

This bring their file to your computer. Verify that you have the file with the **ls** command or view the file in a KDE window.

Did you get their file? Y/N

Troubleshooting

If you have trouble connecting to the FTP site, you need to check the IP address that you type in the browser and the IP address that you have specified in the FTP site properties page. If your network's IP addresses are assigned dynamically with a DHCP server, the IP address might change from time to time. It is a good idea to assign the FTP server a static IP address so that the IP address does not change. I the IP address changes all the time, a lot of administrative overhead will be created because troubleshooting users and customers will be calling and saying that they cannot access the FTP site.

If you have difficulties with the Linux FTP client, try a Windows computer. A Windows system can easily connect to a Linux FTP server by using a popular program called WS_FTP. If you are familiar with WS_FTP, try to connect to the Linux system and download the file directly to the PC.

Reflection

If you set up an FTP server in a business or corporate network, you will have routers and firewalls that you need to configure to allow FTP access to the FTP server. You will also need to take into account that the IP address of the FTP server might not be a public IP address and, therefore, will not be directly connected to the network. In this case, you need to configure the router to forward incoming FTP requests to the proper computer on which your FTP server resides. Remember that the IP address of the web or FTP must be statically assigned.

Lab 10.4.4: Configuring Telnet in Linux

Estimated Time: 25 Minutes

Objective

In this lab, you configure Telnet services on your system so that you can remotely administer your Linux server.

Equipment

The following equipment is required for this exercise:

- System running Linux Red Hat 7.2 or greater
- Another system, either Linux or Windows, to attempt to telnet into the Linux server

Scenario

You are setting up a Linux Server that you need to administer and access remotely. To do this, you decide to install Telnet services on your Linux Red Hat 7.2 computer so that you can gain access to your computer from remote locations.

Procedures

In Linux Red Hat 7.2, the Telnet services are not started by default. In this lab, you navigate to the configuration file first to start the Telnet services. Second, you need to make sure that you have the proper accounts created to access your server through Telnet. In the last part of the lab, you test the Telnet services to confirm that you installed and started the Telnet services properly on your server.

Step 1: Configuring Telnet Services

1. Log in with the root account. You also want to make sure that you are at the CLI command prompt. If you are in the KDE interface, open a terminal emulator window.

2. From a terminal window, type the following:

```
cd/etc/xinetd.d
```

This changes you to the directory where the Telnet configuration file is located.

3. Next, type the following:

```
ls
```

This displays a list of all the configuration files in the xinetd.d directory (see Figure 10-38).

Figure 10-38   Contents of the xinetd.d Directory

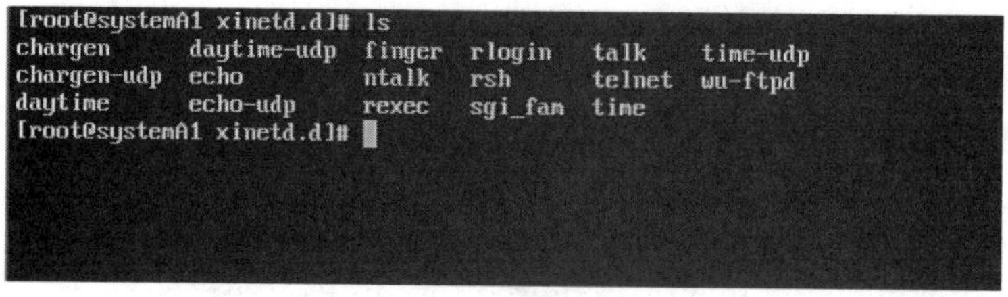

```
[root@systemA1 xinetd.d]# ls
chargen      daytime-udp  finger   rlogin   talk      time-udp
chargen-udp  echo         ntalk    rsh      telnet    wu-ftpd
daytime      echo-udp     rexec    sgi_fam  time
[root@systemA1 xinetd.d]#
```

4. Locate the Telnet file. Is it present? Y/N

5. Check the confirmation of the Telnet file; type the following:

   vi telnet

   This allows you to use the vi Editor to change the Telnet configuration file.

6. After the vi editor window opens, press **i** on the keyboard to enter Insert mode. Locate the disable = yes line in the configuration file. Use your arrow keys on the keyboard to move the cursor to delete the word yes and replace it with no. This changes the configuration file to allow Telnet access to your server.

   Figure 10-39 shows an example of the Telnet configuration file, with disable changed to no.

Figure 10-39   Configuring Telnet Access

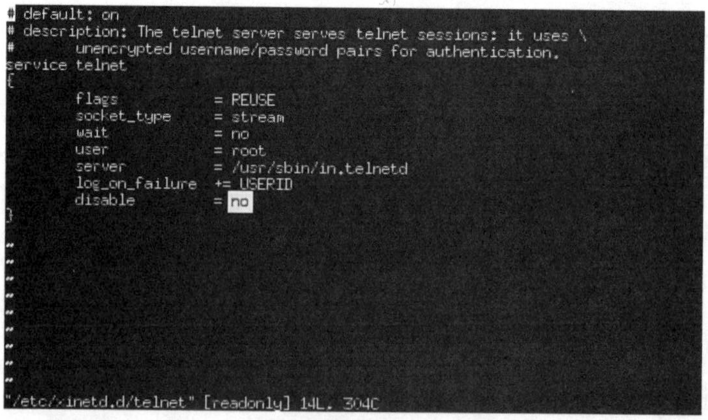

```
# default: on
# description: The telnet server serves telnet sessions: it uses \
#              unencrypted username/password pairs for authentication.
service telnet
{
        flags           = REUSE
        socket_type     = stream
        wait            = no
        user            = root
        server          = /usr/sbin/in.telnetd
        log_on_failure  += USERID
        disable         = no
}

"/etc/xinetd.d/telnet" [readonly] 14L, 304C
```

7. To exit the vi Editor, press **Esc;** then press the : key and type **wq**. This saves the changes that you have made.

Step 2: Starting the Telnet xinetd Daemon

1. Before testing the Telnet service, make sure that the Telnet daemon is running. The daemon that runs the Telnet services is called xinetd (the same daemon that worked with FTP). From the command prompt, type the following:

```
/etc/rc.d/init.d/xinetd stop
```

2. Next, start the xinetd daemon; type the following:

```
/etc/rc.d/init.d/xinetd start
```

3. Check the status of the xinetd daemon; type the following:

```
/etc/rc.d/init.d/xinetd status
```

In the following space write down the status of the xinetd daemon

_____

_____

_____

_____

Step 3: Testing Telnet Access to the Localhost

1. To test Telnet services, type the following:

```
telnet localhost
```

This uses your system to access the Telnet services on your system.

At this point, the system attempts to telnet to your system through the local loopback address 127.0.0.1. It runs through the login procedure and prompts you to enter a username and password.

2. You cannot log in to a remote site with the root account. Use one of the other student accounts to log on and test the Telnet configuration.

If you get a connection to the system, you successfully configured your Linux Red Hat Server for Telnet access.

What directory are you in? Type the following:

```
pwd
```

In the following space, write down the current working directory:

_____

Figure 10-40 shows an example of a Telnet session to the localhost while running the **pwd** command.

Figure 10-40 **pwd** *Command*

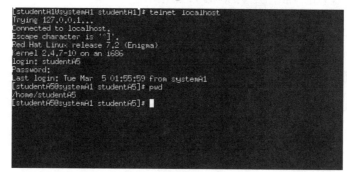

Step 4: Connecting to Other Systems Through Telnet (Optional)

1. As in the FTP lab, use the **ifconfig** command to get your IP address. Exchange IP addresses with a classmate.

Telnet to her computer and have her Telnet to yours. You cannot Telnet using the root account. Use a student account created in previous labs.

3. You can also use an MS Windows computer to telnet to a Linux computer. The example below shows the output of the command line in a Windows computer. To telnet from a Windows computer, go to **Start/Run**; type **telnet** and the IP address (see Figure 10-41).

Figure 10-41   Telnet Access from MS-Windows Start/Run

When prompted, type in the correct user account and password. You should see the results in Figure 10-42.

Figure 10-42   Successful Telnet Connection

Troubleshooting

Configuring services such as Telnet for a Linux operating system can be somewhat confusing to the inexperienced user. Editing the configuration files can be a difficult task, so it is important to remember where these files are located and how to navigate to them. Telnet can be a useful troubleshooting tool, which allows you to gain access to your system from virtually any operating system that has an Internet connection. As a system administrator, this can help you with your troubleshooting efforts.

Reflection

What security risks does enabling Telnet pose to your system?

_____

_____

_____

1. What are some precautions that allow you to provide security while having Telnet access enabled on your system?

_____

_____

_____

_____

Lab 10.4.5: Creating a Samba Server

Estimated Time: 25 Minutes

Objective

In this lab, you configure a Linux server as a Samba file server to provide access from Windows clients.

Equipment

The following equipment is required for this exercise:

- Computer with Linux Red Hat 7.x installed

- Computer with Windows 2000 installed that is on the same network as the Linux computer

Scenario

You are the system administrator of a large company and you have many Windows client workstations that employees use. These Windows clients need access to the Linux file servers to back up their data and have access to network shared files.

Procedures

Step 1: Adding a Samba User

Note: Log in as the root user prior to starting this lab.

Adding a Samba user account is similar to adding a regular user account.

1. The first thing you need to do is add the user account for the user that needs access to the Linux file server. To do this, enter the following command at the shell prompt:

```
useradd -m johnd
```

2. Next, assign a password for the new user account. To do this, enter the following command at the shell prompt:

```
passwd johnd
```

When you enter this command, the operating system returns a message stating that it is changing the password for the johnd user account. It then asks you to enter the new password and to retype the password for verification. Do these steps; then proceed to the next step. If you need to add more Samba user accounts, repeat Steps 1 and 2 for all the accounts you need to add.

3. The next step involves creating the Samba password file. To do this, enter the following command at the command prompt:

```
cat /etc/passwd | /usr/bin/mksmbpasswd.sh > /etc/samba/passwd
```

4. Next, you need to add an SMB password for users that have Samba accounts. To do this, enter the following commands at the shell prompt:

```
smbpasswd johnd
```

When you enter this command, the operating system returns a message stating that it is changing the SMB password for the johnd user account. It then asks you to enter the new password and to retype the password for verification. Do these steps and proceed to the next step.

Step 2: Starting the Samba Service

1. To start the SMB daemon, enter the following command at the shell prompt:

```
/etc/init.d/smb/ start
```

This command runs the Samba service during the current session, but after the system is rebooted, the Samba service will be turned off.

2. To start the Samba service automatically every time the system is rebooted, enter the following command at the shell prompt:

```
/sbin/chkconfig smb on
```

This command forces the Samba service to start automatically in run levels 3, 4, and 5. At this point, you can go to any Windows system and map a network drive to the user's home directory for the user account you just created. To map a network drive, use the following syntax from a Windows system:

```
//Linux servername/username
```

Reflection

What are some of the advantages to creating a share like this for Windows systems? Do any security concerns need to be addressed?

_____

_____

_____

_____

_____

Lab 10.4.9: Writing a Script File in Linux

Estimated Time: 25 Minutes

Objective

In this lab, you learn to create a script file and run it in the Linux environment.

Equipment

To complete this lab you need the following equipment:

- Lab computer with Linux installed and running
-

Scenario

The members of the engineering department are working on some important documents that need to be backed up frequently. This involves a repetitive process that requires them to type a long list of commands every time they need to perform a backup. Instead of typing all these different commands individually each time, you decide to write a script file to execute all of them with one command.

Procedures

This lab requires basic knowledge of the command line and the vi Editor. In the first step of this lab, you log on to the system with the root account and create the script. In Step 2 of the lab, you assign permissions on the script so that only the specified users can execute it. Then in Step 3 of this lab, you log in with the studentXX account and execute the script.

Background on the Linux .tar and .gz Extensions

When you see a .tar (tape archive) file extension, someone has bundled two or more files together—usually for backup purposes. When you see a .gz extension, the file has been compressed—this is similar to the .zip extension in DOS.

For example, to archive a folder of WordPerfect files in a wp directory, use the following command:

```
tar -cvf mywpdocs.tar wp/
```

To see all the files, use the following command:

    `tar -tvf mywpdocs.tar`   (the –t will list all the files)

To extract all the files, use the following command:

    `tar -xvf mywpdocs.tar`   (the –x extracts the contents)

The following is a list of flags used with the .tar command:

-c	Create a new archive
-t	List the contents of an archive
-x	Extract the contents
-f	Write the archive to file
-M	Span multiple floppies if the archive is too big for one floppy
-v	List the files as they are being processed
-u	Add files to the archive
-z	Compress or decompress automatically

gzip and gunzip

It is common for files to be compressed when a tar archive is created:

- **gzip mywpdocs.tar** creates a compressed file called mywpdocs.tar.gz and the original file will be deleted.

- **gunzip mywpdocs.tar.gz** decompresses the file.

-

Step 1: Creating the Script

1. Log in with the studentxx account and make sure that you are in your home directory. (Ask your instructor for the correct login for your computer.) At the command prompt, type the following:

`mkdir mybkup`

`cd mybkup`

`touch file1 file2 file3`

This creates a small subdirectory in the /home directory called mybkup, which contain three files. Verify the creation of the three files with the **ls** command; type the following:

`ls`

Were file1, file2, and file3 created in the mybkup directory? Y/N

Return to the home directory; type the following:

```
cd
```

2. Create a vi script that will automate the backup process. From the command line, type the following:

```
vi/home/studentA5/backup
```

This launches the vi text editor and a file called backup will be created and saved in the home directory.

3. After the vi Editor is open, type the letter **i** on your keyboard to enter the text Insert mode.

4. Type the following text into the text editor:

```
#!/bin/sh
#
ls -R mybkup
tar -cvf mybkup > mybkup.tar
ls -l
#
```

To exit and save the file, press the **Esc** key and the colon (:) on your keyboard. Type the following:

```
Wq
```

5. Verify that the backup script exists; at the command prompt, type the following:

```
ls
```

Does the file backup exist in this directory? Y/N

6. Verify the contents of the backup script; at the command prompt, type the following:

```
cat backup
```

Do the contents of the backup file match Step 4?

Step 2: Assigning Permissions

1. For a script to be executable, the file permissions need to be changed. At the command prompt, type the following:

```
chmod 700 backup
```

2. To check the permissions of the backup file type:

```
ls -l backup
```

Write the results in the following space:

_____

_____

How do you know that the file is now executable?

_____

_____

Step 3: Executing the Script

1. At the command prompt, execute the script; type the following:

```
/home/studentA5/backup
```

2. Verify that a new file was created after the script was executed; type the following:

```
ls
```

Does a file called mybkup.tar now exist in the home directory? Y/N

Step 4: Deleting and Recovering the mybkup Directory

1. From the /home/studentA5 directory, locate the original mybkup file; type the following:

```
ls -R mybkup
```

Is the directory mybkup there? Y/N

2. Delete the mybkup directory; type the following:

```
rm -fr mybkup
```

3. Verify that the mybkup directory has been deleted; type the following:

```
ls mybkup
```

Is the directory gone? Y/N

4. Recover the mybkup directory with the **tar** command; type the following:

```
tar -xvf mybkup.tar
```

5. Verify that the original directory has been restored with the backup; type the following:

```
ls -R mybkup
```

6. Is the directory there and are file1, file2 and file3 there? Y/N.

In the following space, list the directories and files in your home directory:

_____

_____

Did you get your directory and files back? Y/N

Worksheet 11.1.1: Overview of Backup Methods

1. One of the most important duties of a system administrator is to protect important
   _____ on network servers.

2. The priorities of storage devices are not that they be fast or easily accessible but rather
   the following:

   a. _____

   b. _____

   c. _____

   d. _____

3. Commonly used backup devices include the following:

   a. _____

   b. _____

   c. _____

   d. _____

4. Define the following terms:

   Full Backup

   _____

   _____

   _____

   Partial Backup

   _____

   _____

   _____

   Incremental Backup

   _____

   _____

   _____

   Differential Backup

   _____

   _____

   _____

5. Explain the difference between a Copy and a Daily backup.

   _____

   _____

   _____

   _____

Worksheet 11.1.3: Types of Backup Hardware

1. What is the most common hardware device used for backup operations?

   _____

2. How important is a backup device on a network that has mission critical data on its servers and why?

   _____

   _____

3. What two types of tapes use the helical scan hardware much like a VCR?

   _____

4. List the different types of DDS formats and their compression capacity.

   _____

   _____

5. What companies developed Linear Tape-Open (LTO) technology? What is the difference between the two forms of LTO?

   _____

   _____

   _____

6. What tape format has the fastest transfer speed?

   _____

7. What tape format can hold the most information?

   _____

Match the available answers to the following questions. Answers can be used more than once.

| A—Tape Autochangers | B—Tape Arrays | C—Tape Libraries |
| D—Disk Drivers | E—(CD-R) | F—(CD-RW) |

8. These two devices use compact disks to store data and are relatively slow backup devices: _____, _____.

9. Another name for tape auto loader is _____.

10. Uses tapes to add fault tolerance by using the tape version of RAID characteristics _____.

11. This device relieves the operator from having to remove old tapes and put in new ones _____.

12. This device stores tens or hundreds of tapes and can automatically locate and load them when needed _____.

13. Compared to a tape drive backup, _____ are considerably faster.

14. Hot swappable and offsite storage are two key components of _____.

Worksheet 11.1.4: Environmental Guidelines for a Server Room

1. Name two items that cause interference with electric pull, and which you do not want to place your server next to: _____ , _____

2. The space above a drop ceiling (between the ceiling and the floor of a building's next level) is called the _____.

3. _____ cable uses _____ _____ as the external covering that gives off poisonous fumes when burned.

4. The temperature in a server room should be between _____ to _____.

5. The storage temperature should be between _____ to _____.

6. What increases when humidity is low or not present in the server room?

_____

7. Why is air quality so important to the server room?

_____

_____

8. List a few ways that a fire can be extinguished in a server room environment without destroying all the equipment:

_____

_____

9. What do the different lettering codes stand for on a fire extinguisher?

Code A: _____

Code B: _____

Code C: _____

Code D: _____

If you work in a known flood plain, what two things should you have in place?
_____ , _____.

What kinds of information can the hardware management card tell the administrator?
_____ , _____ , _____ , _____

Lab 11.1.5a: Backing Up with Windows 2000

Estimated Time: 20 Minutes

Objective

In this lab, you use the Backup Wizard from Windows 2000 to perform a backup of files to your hard disk.

Equipment

The following equipment is required for this exercise:

- Computer system running Windows 2000 Professional

Scenario

You are the System Administrator for the XYZ Company and you need to back up some of the files on the server. Losing these files would cause damage to the company. It is your job to perform backups as preventative maintenance and to back up important files as required.

Procedures

In this lab, you use the Windows Backup Wizard to select the files that you want to back up and then perform the backup.

Step 1: Creating, Running, and Verifying a Backup Job

1. Log on to the server with the Administrator account.

2. When the system boots up, go **to Start** > **Run**.

3. In the Run Dialog box, type **ntbackup** and click **OK**. The Backup dialog box displays.

Figure 11-1   **ntbackup** *Command*

4. Read the three descriptions under the Welcome tab, and click **Backup Wizard**. The Backup Wizard starts.

Figure 11-2   Windows 2000 Backup Tool

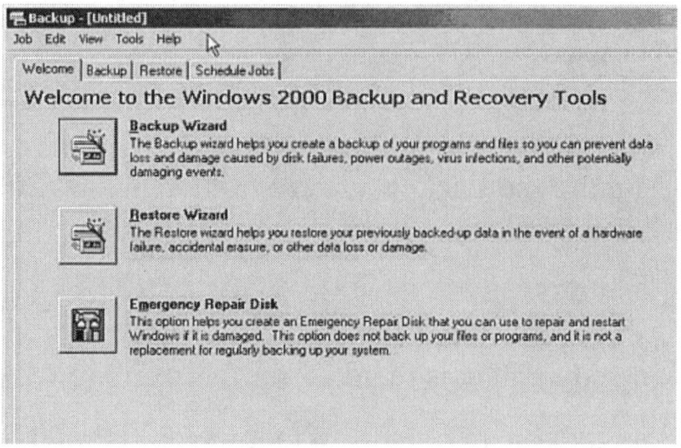

Figure 11-3   Windows 2000 Backup Wizard

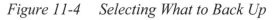

5. Click **Next** to display the What to Back Up screen. Select the type of backup you want to perform.

Figure 11-4   Selecting What to Back Up

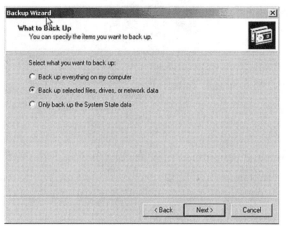

6. Click the **Back up selected files, drives, or network data** button and click **Next**. At this point, the Items to Back Up screen displays, prompting you to select the local and network drives, folders, and files to be backed up.

Figure 11-5   Selecting Items to Back Up

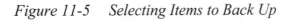

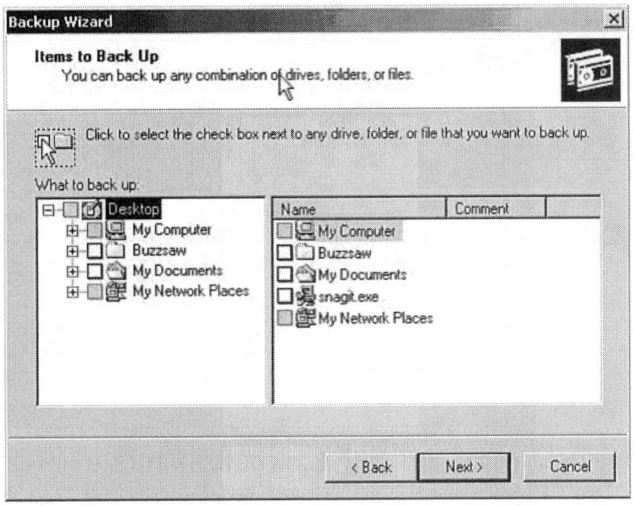

7. Expand My Computer and double-click the words **System State** (Do not select the box to the left of System State.) to display the System State files that can be backed up.

Figure 11-6   Selecting System State to Back Up

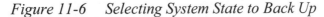

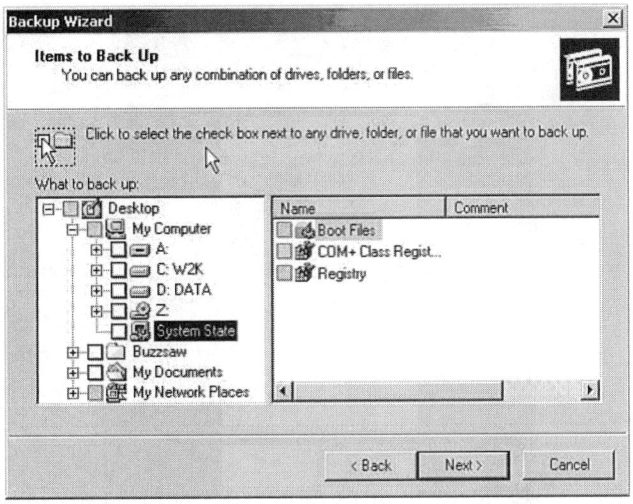

8. In the left window, expand the C: drive by double-clicking the letter **C**. (Do not select the check box to the left of C:).

Figure 11-7   Selecting Items to Back Up

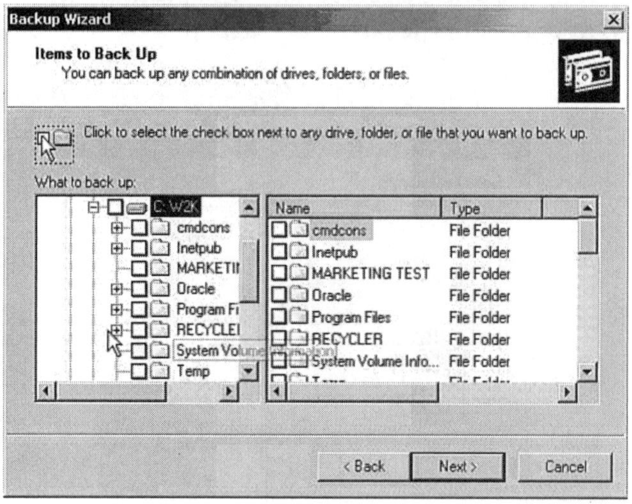

9. In the details window, scroll down and select the **boot.ini** check box and click **Next**. The Where to Store the Backup screen will display. In the Backup Media or File Name text box, type **c:\backup1.bkf** and click **Next**.

Figure 11-8   Selecting the boot.ini File to Back Up

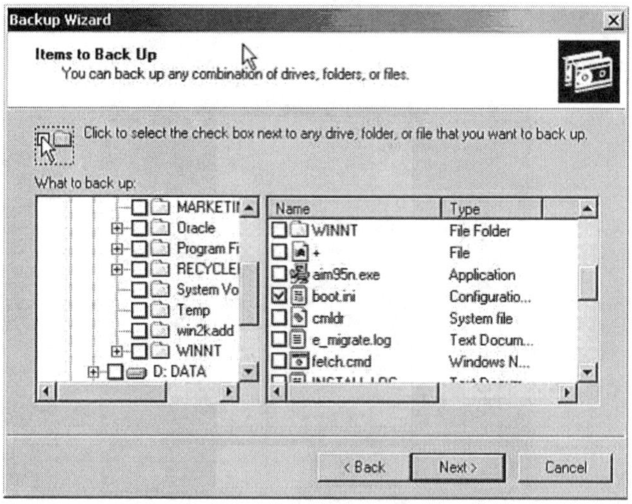

Note: The Backup Media Type drop-down list will be gray because you do not have any removable media to back up to and File is the only backup media type available. In a real scenario, you would want to back up to some type of removable media, removable disk, or to another hard drive on another computer. For the purpose of this lab, you are backing up on the same drive.

10. The Completing the Backup Wizard screen displays. This screen shows the details of the backup job that you will perform; you can also continue to make additional changes from this point. Click the **Advanced** button.

Figure 11-9   Completing the Backup Wizard

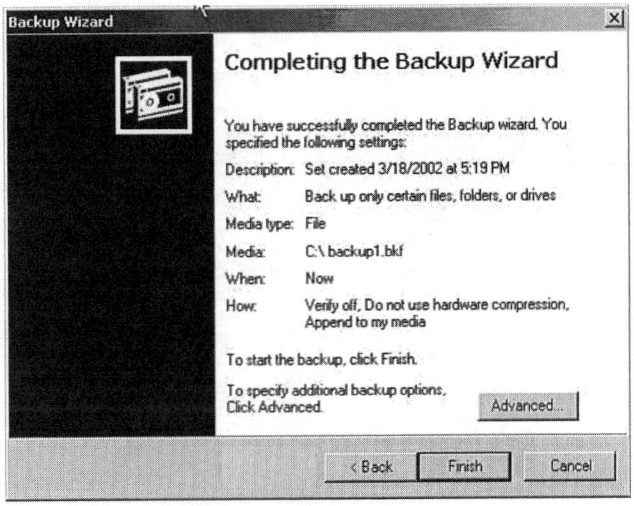

11. When the Type of Backup screen displays, make sure that **Normal** is selected and that the **Backup Migrated Remote Storage Data** check box is not checked.

Figure 11-10   Selecting the Type of Backup

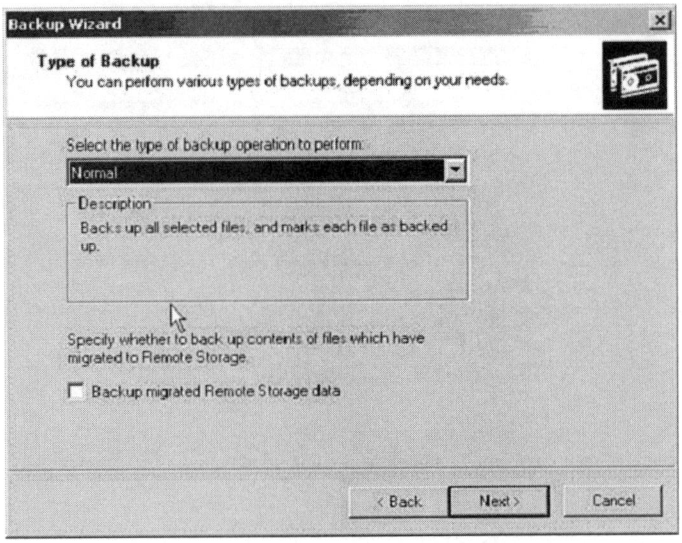

12. Click **Next**. The How to Backup screen should display. This allows you to verify the backed up data after performing the backup.

13. Select the **Verify data after backup** check box and click **Next**.

Figure 11-11   How to Back Up

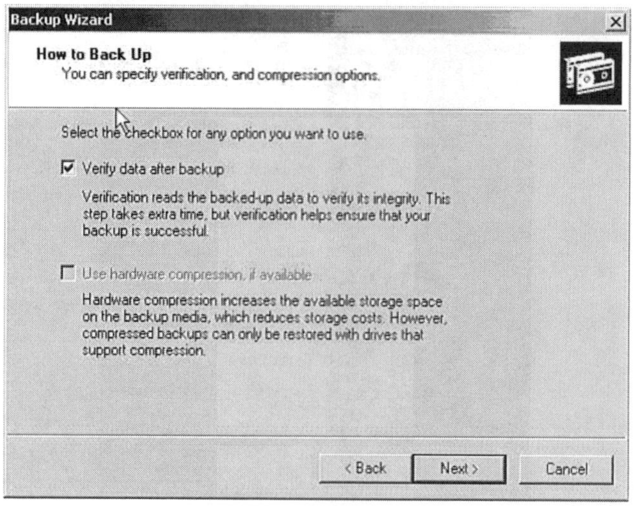

14. The Media Options page displays, which prompts you to specify whether to append this backup job to existing media or to overwrite existing backup data on the destination media. Click **Replace the data on the media with this backup** button.

Figure 11-12   Media Options

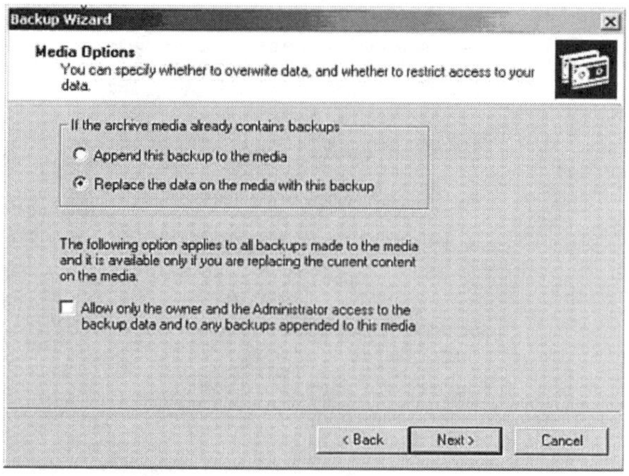

15. Click **Next**. The Backup Label screen displays asking you to supply a label for the backup job and for the backup media. If you do not enter the label information, Windows supplies a backup label and media label by using the current date and time by default.

16. In the Backup Label text box, type **Boot.ini backup set created on xxx** (**xxx** is today's date and time). Do not change anything in the Media Label text box and click **Next**.

235

Figure 11-13   Backup Label

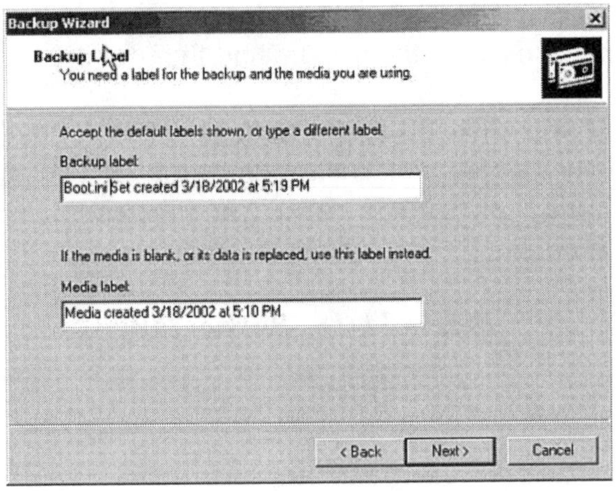

17. The When to Back Up screen displays. Choose whether to run the backup job now or schedule this backup job. For this lab, select the **Now** radio button. Click **Next**.

Figure 11-14   When to Back Up

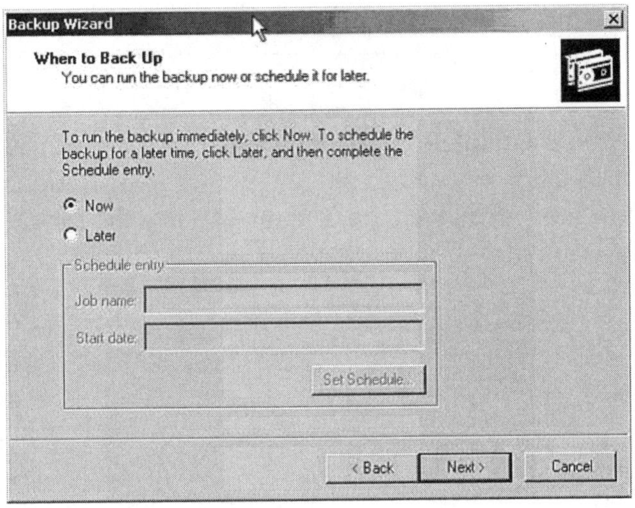

18. When the Completing the Backup Wizard screen displays, click **Finish** to start the backup job.

Figure 11-15   Completing the Backup Wizard

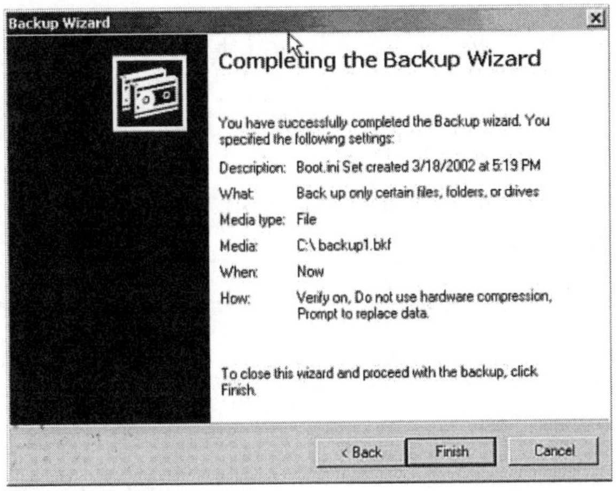

19. Windows Backup displays the Selection Information dialog box, which indicates the estimated amount of data for the backup and the time to complete.

20. The Windows Backup displays the Backup Progress dialog box, which shows the status of the backup operation, statistics on estimated and actual amount of data being processed, the time that has elapsed, and the estimated time that remains for the backup to complete.

Figure 11-16   Backup Progress Indicator

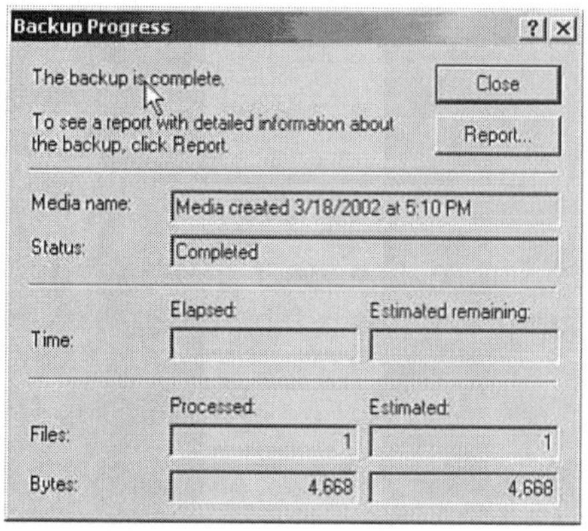

21. When the backup is complete, click the **Report** button. A backup report appears. The backup report contains key details about the backup operation, such as the time it started and how many files were backed up. Review the report and close Notepad.

Figure 11-17   Backup Process Log file

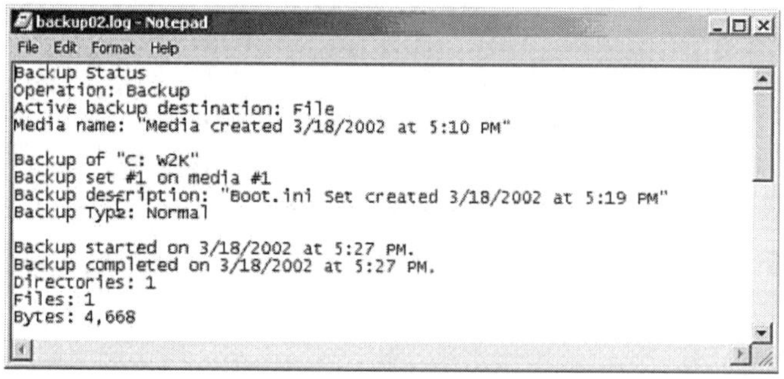

22. Close the Backup Progress dialog box and the Backup Dialog box.

Reflection

This is one way to perform a backup. Are there any other ways that a backup can be performed?

Lab 11.1.5b: Backing Up with Linux

Estimated Time: 20 Minutes

Objective

In this lab, you use the backup utilities provided by the Linux operating system to perform a backup of directories and files on your hard disk.

Equipment

The following equipment is required for this exercise:

- Computer system running Linux Red Hat 7.X

Scenario

You are the System Administrator for the XYZ Company and you need to back up some of the files on the server. Losing these files would cause damage to the company. It is your job to perform backups as preventative maintenance and to back up important files as required.

Procedures

Use the Linux commands to perform a backup procedure on the files that you want to back up. First, make a directory and create files in that directory. You then back up the files and verify that the action was successful.

Step 1: Creating the Directories and Files

1. Make sure that you are in your home directory. To verify this, type **pwd** at the command prompt and press **Enter**. Are you in your home directory? Y/N

   If not, type **cd** at the command prompt. As you recall from previous sections, the **cd** command by itself takes you to your home directory.

2. Next, at the Login command, log in with a student account and open a terminal window.

3. At the command prompt, type **mkdir bakupdir** and press **Enter**. This creates the directory in which you can create the files. Verify with the **ls** command. Is the directory bkupdir there? Y/N

4. Next, type **cd bkupdir** and press **Enter**.

5. Type **touch file_A file_B file_C** and press **Enter**. The **touch** command creates three files. Verify with the **ls** command. Are the three files there? Y/N

6. Type **cd** and press **Enter** to return to your home directory.

7. Next, type **ls - R bkupdir** and press **Enter**. This shows you the directory and the files that you created within the directory.

Step 2: Performing the Backup

1. Next, back up the bkupdir directory. At the command prompt, type **tar –cv bkupdir > bkup.tar** and press **Enter**.

2. Type **ls –l** to confirm that the backup file was created. Is it there? Y/N

3. Type **rm –fr bkupdir** and press **Enter**. The **rm** command deletes the directory and the three files you created.

4. Type **ls –l** and press **Enter** to confirm that the directory was deleted. Is it there? Y/N

5. Next, type **tar –xvf bkup.tar** and press **Enter** to restore the directories and files. The **tar** command runs the backup program to restore the files.

6. Type **ls –l** and press **Enter**.

Did the original directory and its files reappear? Y/N

Worksheet 11.2.4: Drive Mapping

1. A useful tool that allows an administrator to share resources that are stored on a server is _____.

2. Mapping a network drive in the Windows NOS is easy. You can do it in one of two ways:

   a. _____

   b. _____

3. When you map a drive with Windows Explorer, the mapped drive shows up as _____ in the left pane of Explorer, along with your floppy and CD-ROM drives and hard disk partitions.

4. Another way to map a drive in Windows operating systems uses the _____ path.

5. To map a network drive to the shared resource, enter the following at the command prompt:

   _____

6. What are the two ways that drive mapping can be done with Linux?

   a. _____

   b. _____

7. The Samba daemon would load the _____, which allows communication between Linux and Windows computers.

8. When mapping a drive to a Linux/Unix share from another Linux computer, the following syntax is used:

   _____

9. As with Linux, mapping a drive to a share on a NetWare server can be done with

   _____.

10. You also can map a drive at the command line by using the **map** command. The syntax is as follows:

    _____

    _____

Lab 11.4.5: Checking Resource Usage on Windows 2000

Estimated Time: 20 Minutes

Objective

In this lab, you use the system performance tool to monitor the resource usage on your computer system.

Equipment

The following equipment is required for this exercise:

- Computer system with Windows 2000 Professional installed

Scenario

You arrive at work in the morning and discover that the server seems to be running slow. You decide to open the system's performance monitor to inspect the resource usage on the system. Your options are to upgrade or add another server if the system's resources have been used up.

Procedures

Open the performance monitor and inspect the system resource usage by graphing, and then analyze the graph to decide what might be causing the system to run slowly and what might need to be upgraded.

Step 1: Gathering Information

1. Open the performance monitor. Click **Start** > **Programs** > **Administrative Tools** > **Performance**.

Figure 11-18 System Performance

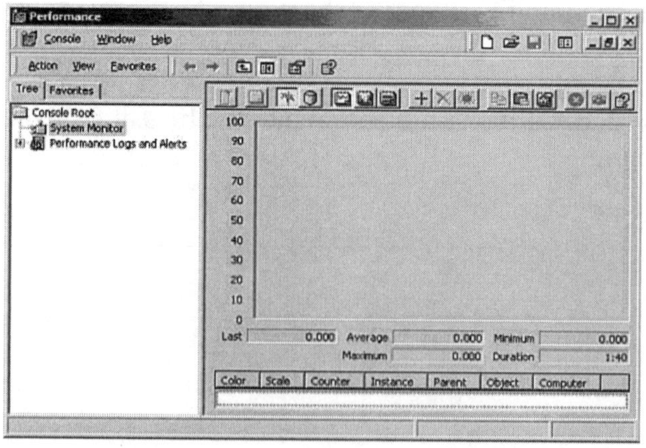

2. Right-click in the right windows and select **Add Counters**.

1

Figure 11-19   Adding Counters

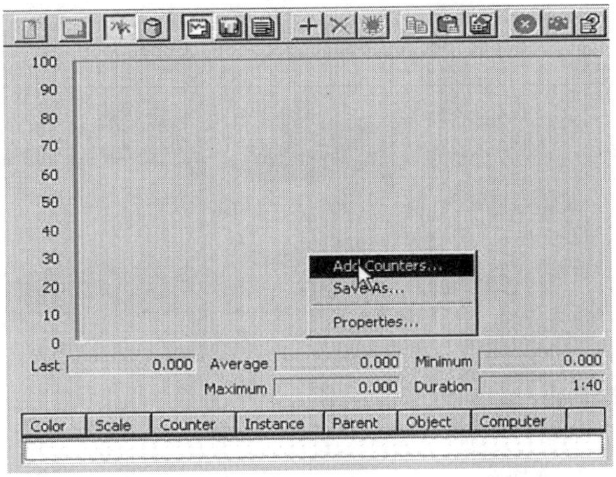

3. Check to make sure **Add Counters** in the performance object drop-down box **Processor** is selected.

4. Select the **Counters from the list** radio button.

Figure 11-20   Adding Counters

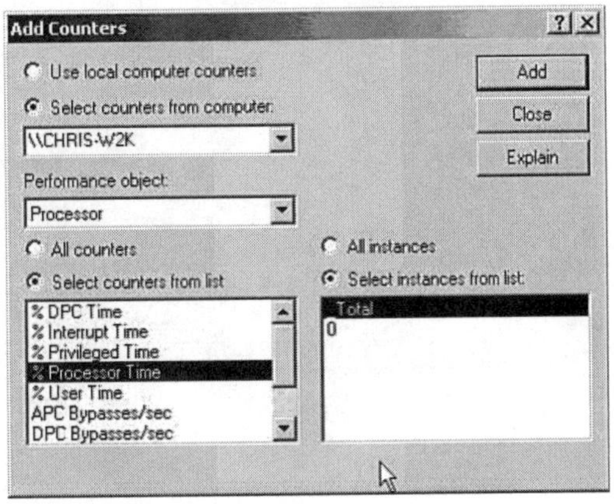

5. While holding the Control key down, use your mouse to select **%Interrupt Time**, **%Processor Time**, **%User Time**, and the **Interrupts/sec**.

Figure 11-21   Adding Counters

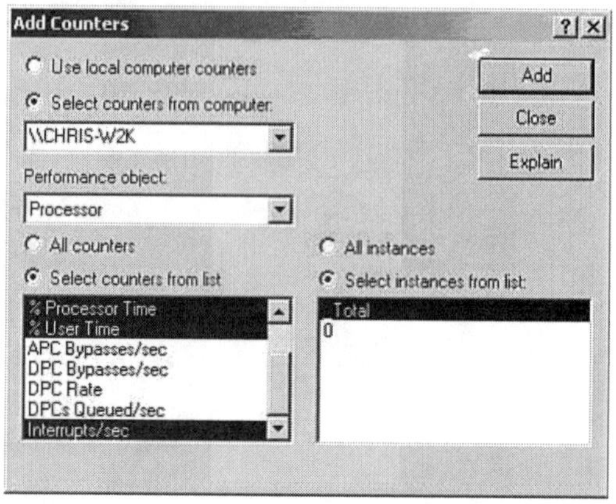

6. Click **Add** and close the box.

7. Let the graph make a pass across the screen at least once, right-click in the graph area, and select **Save As**. Save this file as: Lab Processor Graph. (While this is happening, open up and close some programs to generate some activity on your system.)

Figure 11-22   Saving Changes

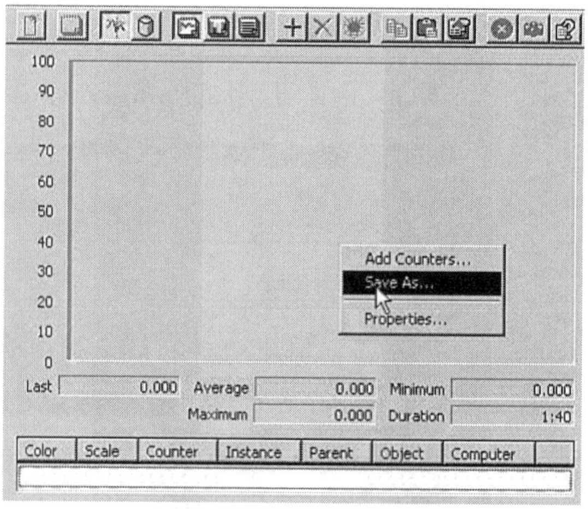

8. Locate the X in the menu bar across the top and delete the **%Interrupt Time**, **%Processor Time**, **%User Time**, and the **Interrupts/sec** monitors.

Figure 11-23   Saving Changes

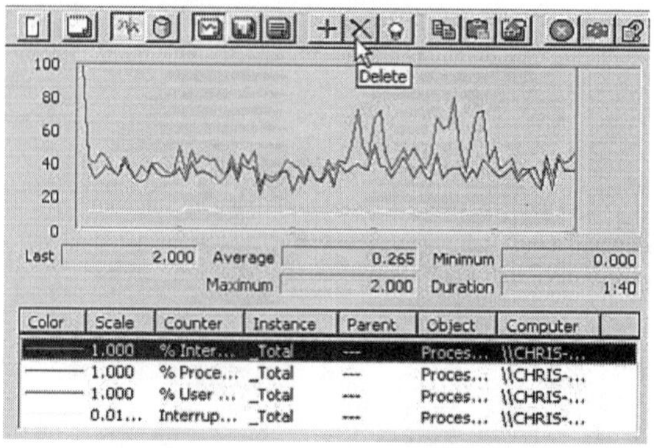

9. Right-click in the right windows and select **Add Counters**.

10. Go back to the performance object drop-down box and select **System**.

Figure 11-24   Adding Counters

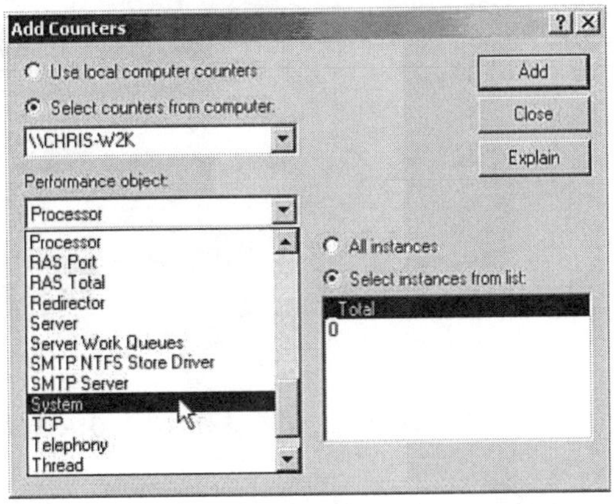

11. While holding the Control key down, use your mouse to select **Processes** and **Threads**.

Figure 11-25   Adding Counters

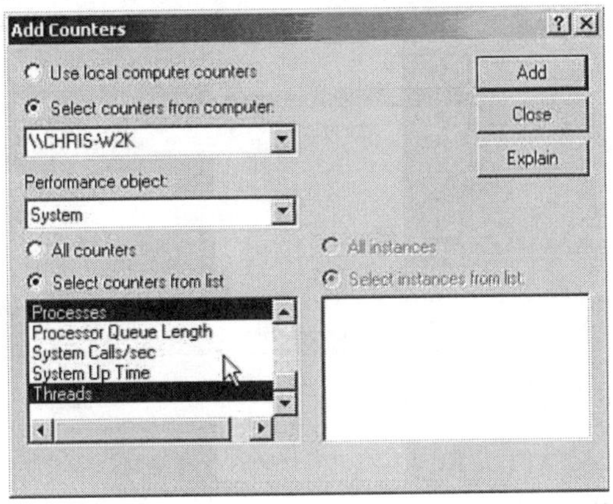

12. Click **Add** and close the box.

13. Let the graph make a pass across the screen at least once, right-click in the graph area, and select **Save As**. Save this file as Lab System Graph.

14. Locate the X in the menu bar across the top and delete the **Processes** and **Threads** monitors.

Figure 11-26 Counter Output

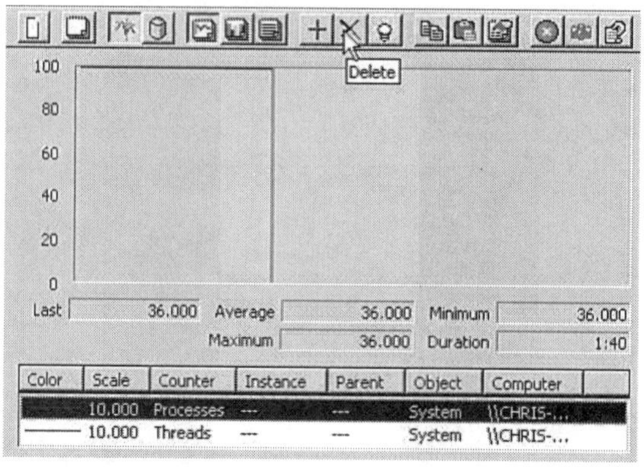

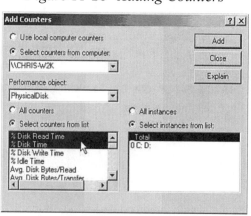

15. Right-click in the right windows and select **Add Counters**.

16. Go back up to the performance object drop-down box and select **Physical Disk**.

Figure 11-27 Adding Counters

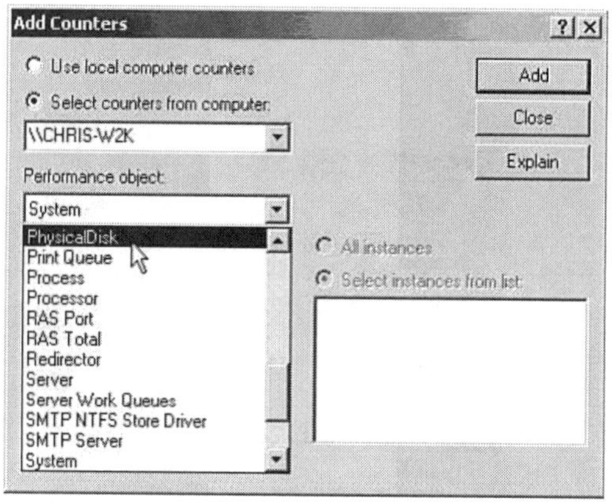

17. While holding the Control key down, use your mouse to select **%Disk Read Time** and **%Disk Write Time**.

Figure 11-28 Adding Counters

18. Click **Add** and close the box.

19. Let the graph make a pass across the screen at least once, right-click in the graph area, and select **Save As**. Save this file as Lab Physical Disk Graph.

20. Locate the X in the menu bar across the top and delete the **%Disk Read Time** and **%Disk Write Time** monitors. (While this is happening, open up and close some programs to generate some activity on your system.)

21. Close the Performance Monitor.

Step 2: Evaluating the Information

1. Navigate to the folder where you saved the performance monitor files.

2. Open them up one by one and analyze them.

3. What conclusions can be drawn from these graphs?

4. What are some reasons for using such graphs?

Troubleshooting

These performance monitor tools can be helpful in troubleshooting your system. They can provide a lot of information about your system and the overall health of your system. By using the performance monitor to check your system's resources, you can effectively evaluate what might be causing problems in your system.

Lab 11.4.6: Checking Resource Usage in Linux

Estimated Time: 20 Minutes

Objective

In this lab, you learn how to check the resources on a Linux system. This lab covers the following commands:

df

du

top

Equipment

The following equipment is required for this exercise:

- Computer with Linux Red Hat 7.2 (or greater) installed

Scenario

You have a server running Linux that has been running efficiently for a long time, and you are worried that the system's resources might be reaching their limits. You decide to run a few of the commands to check the system's resources to ensure that the system runs properly.

Procedures

You use three basic Linux commands to check and record the resource usage on a Linux system.

Step 1: The df Command (Disk File System)

1. Log in as the root user. If you are in the GUI interface, open a terminal window.

2. For information on the **df** command, use the **man df** command; type the following:

```
man df
```

3. In the following space, give a brief description of the **df** command.

_____

4. What does the **–h** switch do?

_____

5. Determine the amount of hard drive space that is being used by Linux; type the following:

```
df
```

To make the output of the **df** command easier to read, type the following:

```
df -h
```

Record your results in the following table:

Filesystem	Size	Used	Avail	Use%	Mounted on

*Figure 11-29 The **df –h** Command*

```
[root@systemA1 boot]# df -h
Filesyem      Size  Used  Avail  Use%  Mounted on
/dev/hda2     1.9G  827M   1.0G   45%  /
/dev/hda1      30M  2.7M    26M   10%  /boot
none           62M     0    61M    0%  /dev/shm
[root@systemA1 boot]#
```

Step 2: The du Command (Disk Usage)

1. Remain logged in as the root user; you need root privileges to gain information about the /etc directory. Use the **man** command to learn about the **du** command. From a terminal window type the following:

   ```
   man du
   ```

2. In the following space give a brief description of the **du** command.

   _____

3. What does the **–h** switch do?

   _____

4. What does the **–s** switch do?

   _____

5. Go to a student home page and type the following:

   ```
   cd /home studentA5
   ```

   Note: The home directory studentA5 is an example only. Use the student account that your instructor has assigned for you.

6. From within the studentA5 home directory, type the following:

   ```
   du
   ```

   Next type the following:

   ```
   du -hs
   ```

   What is the difference between the commands when the **–hs** switches are added? How much space is being used in studentA5's home directory?

The **du** command can be useful in determining the size of any directory or file within a directory. Go to the /etc directory and determine the size of the directory and the size of the passwd file. Type the following command sequence:

```
cd /etc

du

du -hs

du -hs passwd
```

What is the size of the /etc directory?

_____

What is the size of the passwd file?

_____

Figure 11-30 **du** *Command*

Step 3: The top Command

1. Use the **man** command to learn about the **top** command. From a terminal window type the following:

```
man top
```

In the following space, give a brief description of the **top** command.

_____

From a terminal, type the following:

```
top
```

In the following space, write in information determined from the **top** output:

CPU idle time in %	
Number of users	
Number of processes	
Amount of memory	
Amount of memory free	

Figure 11-31 shows an example of the **top** command.

Figure 11-31 **top** *Command*

Troubleshooting

Network administrators use the **top** command to determine system processes. If one application takes too many system resources, it might be a runaway application. How can you identify the application pid (process id)?

_____

_____

Reflection

Monitoring system resources is an issue that network administrators must respond to daily. Develop a plan to track the resources of your Linux systems. Can you automate your plan? How?

_____

_____

Worksheet 11.5.2: Bottlenecks

1. What is a bottleneck?

   _____

2. What effect can a bottleneck have on a network? Give some examples of bottlenecks.

   _____

   _____

3. What are some performance monitoring software utilities for Windows 2000 and Unix/Linux?

   _____

4. When watching the processor or performance monitor what do you look for?

   _____

5. What are the solutions to a processor with a high use percentage?

   _____

6. How can you solve a memory bottleneck?

   _____

7. What are some initial signs of a memory bottleneck?

   _____

8. At what percent does the disk subsystem pose a bottleneck? _____

9. List the first three steps to resolving a disk performance problem?

   _____

   _____

   _____

10. What is the more costly approach to fixing a disk subsystem bottleneck?

   _____

11. At what percentage is network use considered high? _____

12. Would the following scenario solve the network subsystem problem?

  Scenario: You want to make your network subsystem faster after you realize a bottleneck. You are running a 10-Mbps Ethernet network over CAT 3 wire. You believe higher transmission speeds will solve the problem, so you upgrade to 100-Mbps NICs and replace all other 10-Mbps hardware with 100-Mbps hardware. Will this solve the bottleneck in the network subsystem? Explain your answer.

  _____
  _____
  _____

13. What are possibilities for upgrading the network to improve speed and thus removing bottlenecks?

  _____
  _____
  _____

Worksheet 11.5.3: Baseline

1. What does a baseline consist of?

_____

2. What is the optimum time to take a baseline reading of your network?

_____

3. What are a few measurements that need to be taken when performing a baseline?

_____

_____

4. What can be done to reduce heavy bandwidth users after they are identified?

_____

_____

5. What network monitoring application can use a lot of bandwidth and should be used during down times?

_____

6. What is mapping of use patterns used for?

_____

7. When is a good time to use network monitoring software?

_____

8. How can you as an administrator find out if employees are gaming or web surfing?

_____

Worksheet 11.5.8: SNMP

1. Using TCP/IP what port does SNMP run by default? _____

2. When using SNMP, what can you remotely monitor?

_____

3. What kind of information can be found when using SNMP?

   1) _____

   2) _____

   3) _____

   4) _____

4. Add _____ to the IP address resolution for the computers that you are setting up with SNMP.

5. Using SNMP, what systems can be monitored to gather information?

   1) _____

   2) _____

   3) _____

   4) _____

   5) _____

   6) _____

6. What third-party network management software is available?

   1) _____

   2) _____

   3) _____

7. What are the two main parts to SNMP?

_____, _____

8. You need at least one management system to use the SNMP Service? True/False

9. What is the management system responsible for?

_____

_____

_____

10. What are the generic commands used with the management system and what do they do?

1) _____ definition:

_____

_____

_____

2) _____ definition:

_____

_____

_____

3) _____ definition:

_____

_____

_____

11. What is a group of hosts known as? _____

12. What is the SNMP agent responsible for?

_____

_____

_____

13. Is the agent an active or passive device responding to a direct query?

_____

14. What is the special case called when the agent is acting on its own without a query?

_____

_____

_____

Lab 11.5.10: Installing SNMP

Estimated Time: 20 Minutes

Objective

In this lab, you set up monitoring agents to run tests and alerts for your system.

Equipment

You need the following items to complete this lab:

- PC with Windows 2000 Professional

Scenario

You are going to monitor the network and you want to install SNMP as the monitoring software.

Procedures

In this lab, you install the SNMP service and configure the agent properties.

Step 1

Click **Start**, point to **Settings**, point to **Control Panel**, and click **Add/Remove Programs**.

Step 2

On the Add/Remove Program window, click **Add/Remove Windows Components.** Wait a few seconds for the wizard to load.

1. What are some of the Windows components that you already have installed on your PC?

_____

Step 3

Put a checkmark in the box next to **Management and Monitoring Tools** and click **Next**.

Step 4

After it is done installing the proper files, click **Finish.** This concludes the installation of SNMP, thus allowing you to monitor network performance.

Step 5

Close all windows. Now that you have installed SNMP, you need to configure the Agent properties in SNMP.

Step 6

Click **Start**> **Programs** > **Administrative Tools** > **Computer Management**. In the console tree, open **Services and Applications** and click **Services**.

Step 7

In the details pane, right-click **SNMP Service** and click **Properties**.

Step 8

Find and click the **Agent** tab, and in the Contact box, type the name of the user or administrator for this computer.

Step 9

In the Location box, type the physical location of the computer or the contact.

Step 10

In the Service box below deselect all the boxes and put a checkmark in the Physical box. You have just configured the SNMP agent properties.

Reflection

List additional SNMP parameters that are configurable through the SNMP Service Properties window?

_____

From an administration standpoint, what are some of the benefits to applying SNMP on the network?

_____

_____

_____

Lab 11.5.11: Configuring SNMP Security and Traps

Estimated Time: 20 Minutes

Objective

In this lab, you configure SNMP monitoring agents to run tests and alerts for your system.

Equipment

You need the following items to complete this lab:

- PC with Windows 2000 Professional
- SNMP needs to be installed

Scenario

You find that your network needs to be monitored more closely and you need to finish setting up SNMP with security and traps.

Procedures

In this lab, you configure the security and traps features used by SNMP.

Step 1

Click **Start> Programs > Administrative Tools > Computer Management**. In the console tree, open **Services and Applications** and click **Services**.

Step 2

In the details pane, right-click **SNMP Service** and click **Properties**.

Step 3

Click the **Security** tab; put a checkmark in the box next to Send authentication trap. (This displays a trap message when the authentication fails.)

Step 4

Click **Add** under Accepted community names. A SNMP Service Configuration box opens. Under Community rights, highlight **READ ONLY;** right-click and then select **What's This**. What are the different definitions?

None

_____

Notify

_____

Read Only

_____

Read Write

_____

Read Create

_____

Next, make the Community Name **public1** and click **Add**.

Step 5

In the lower part of the Security tab window, select **Accept SNMP packet from any host**. Then, click **Apply** and **OK**.

What is the purpose of a community name?

_____

Step 6

From the SNMP Service Properties window, click the **Traps** tab; under Community name, type **public1** in the drop down list and click **Add** to list.

(Public appears in the box by default.)

Step 7

Under Trap destinations, click **Add** and type the **Host name** (the name of your PC) in the box. Then, click **Apply** and **OK** and close all windows.

Troubleshooting

Before configuring SNMP on a network, document the layout of your network depicting SNMP communities. Also, when setting the community name, it is recommended that you do not use the default name of PUBLIC. This poses a security risk because if access is gained to the device, intruders can obtain device information and possibly change the configurations.

Reflection

What is the default SNMP community name? _____

Lab 12.1.4: Using Device Manager in Windows 2000 Server

Estimated Time: 20 Minutes

Objective

Upon completion of this lab, you will be able to navigate Device Manager, locate hardware, and manually reinstall a device.

Equipment

You will need the following items to complete this lab:

- Windows 2000 Professional or Server installed and configured

Scenario

You just installed Windows 2000 Server on your machine, and you want to see if all your devices are working You find that your CD-ROM device is not working properly, so you need to resolve the problem. You will learn how to uninstall and reinstall the device.

Procedures

This lab is going to be broken up into a few sections. First, you will navigate through Device Manager, and then you will reinstall the CD-ROM driver.

Step 1

Right-click **My Computer** and select **Properties**. List the different tabs available in the System Properties window.

_____

_____

Step 2

Next, click the **Hardware** tab. Now, click **Device Manager**. What do you see?

_____

_____

Step 3

Double-click **Keyboards** to display your keyboard. Double-click your keyboard. What is your Device Status?

_____

_____

Step 4

Click the **Resources** tab. List what IRQ the keyboard is using: _____.

Step 5

Locate the CD-ROM device. Double-click **CD-ROM** and you will see your CD-ROM installed on your machine. Double click **CD-ROM**. What tabs are listed and what do they contain?

_____

_____

Step 6

Click the **Drivers** tab. Now, click the **Uninstall** button. Click **OK**. Your computer is now uninstalling the CD-ROM device. When it finishes, look at the CD-ROM device. Is it there? Why?

_____

Step 7

Now, you will reinstall the CD-ROM driver. Click the **Action** button in the Device Manager; click **Scan for Hardware changes**. What happened?

_____   _____

Can you now see your CD-ROM drive in Device Manager?

_____

Reflection

How can using Device Manager be beneficial to an administrator who is troubleshooting the devices connected to the server?

_____

_____

_____

Lab 12.1.5: Using the HCL

Estimated Time: 15 Minutes

Objective

Upon completion of this lab, you will be able to identify and analyze the compatibility of system hardware to the corresponding operating system.

Equipment

You need the following items to complete this lab:

- Internet access

Scenario

You have been assigned the responsibility of loading a network operating system (NOS) onto a server that best supports the existing hardware. Your manager has asked that the NOS be Windows 2000, Linux (Red Hat), or Linux (Caldera).

Procedures

In this lab, you explore the websites of the NOSs listed in preceding "Scenario" section. Four pieces of hardware need to be compatible with the NOS. Compatibility information can be ascertained by using the Hardware Compatibility List (HCL) of each NOS. Each NOS website contains an HCL.

Step 1

Open three instances of an Internet browser.

Step 2

Copy/paste or type each URL into the browser. The websites are as follows:

- **Windows 2000 Server:**

  www.microsoft.com/windows2000/server/howtobuy/upgrading/compat/default.asp

  After you connect, click the **Hardware Devices** tab and start your search.

- **Linux (Red Hat):**

  http://hardware.redhat.com

  After you connect, click **Hardware Compatibility List**, and start your search.

- **Linux (Caldera):**

  www.calderasystems.com/support/hardware/

  After you connect, click **OpenLinux eSERVER 2.3**, and start your search.

Step 3

Using the HCL, gather information concerning the following hardware components. Depending whether the product is supported by the NOS, write yes or no next to each device.

Device	Product	Network Operating Systems		
		Windows 2000	Linux(Red Hat)	Linux(Caldera)
Network Interface Card	3Com Etherlink XL (3c905)			
Video Card	RAGE 128 PRO			
CPU	Pentium III			
Hint:Type, compatable CPU in the "Search This Site" box	AMD K5			
	AMD K6-III			
SCSI	DELL PowerVault 110T LTO			

Step 4

On the Caldera website, what were the three unsupported products listed?

_____

_____

_____

Troubleshooting

If you are experiencing problems with your hardware devices or software devices you should first verify that they are properly connected and installed. If the problem still exists, try restarting your machine. Rebooting the machine refreshes and reloads the hardware drivers. However, if the problem still exists, the driver might need to be updated. The driver can usually be updated by accessing the company's website or homepage of the OS.

Reflection

Which website did you find to be the easiest to navigate and have the information that you were looking for? _____

Which website was the most difficult to navigate? _____

Lab 12.2.3: Updating Your Server's Operating System and Hardware

Estimated Time: 25 Minutes

Objective

Upon completion of this lab, you will be able to upgrade your operating system with the latest patches and updates. Also, you learn how to search the Internet and find different hardware vendor websites and download and install the latest drivers.

Equipment

You need the following items to complete this lab:

- Lab computer with Windows 2000 installed
- Internet access

Scenario

You just installed Windows 2000 on your machine. For the server to run as securely and smoothly as possible, you need to search the Internet for the latest updates and patches. Obtaining these updates is essential for improving and maintaining the server's hardware and software performance. During a post-installation inspection of the devices, you notice that the sound card driver was not properly installed, so you need to install it manually.

Procedures

In the first part of this lab, you deal with updating the operating system. Searching for device updates should start at the manufacturer's website. Usually, the manufacturer's website has the latest updates available. In the second part of the lab, you update the hardware devices. In this lab, you focus on updating the sound card, but this procedure is relatively the same for all hardware devices.

Step 1

Open your web browser and in the URL box type **windowsupdate.microsoft.com**.

Step 2

On the left-hand side of the web page, you can see a box that says *Product Updates*. Click it. A window pops up on the screen that says *Security Warning*. This warning asks if you trust the content from the company that you are downloading from. In this case, you do trust Microsoft, so click **Yes**.

Step 3

When you click the Product updates, Microsoft scans your computer to see what updates you don't have and lists those deficiencies. Choose the update **Windows Critical Update Notification 3.0**, and click the **Download** button. After clicking the Download button, answer the following question and the update automatically downloads and installs itself.

Step 4

You have just updated you server. To download all the updates, repeat the previous steps.

Step 5

Now, you need to download an updated driver for your hardware peripherals. This is a basic instructional process that you can follow for each of your hardware peripherals. You are updating the driver for the soundcard made by Creative.

Step 6

Type in the website www.creative.com and click **North America**. This takes you to the correct web page to download from.

Step 7

Put the mouse pointer over the Support icon and click **Download Drivers**.

Step 8

In the middle of the screen (where it says *Start Here*) is a list of products with available updates from Creative.

What products have updates available on the Creative Labs' website? (List three.)

_____,

_____,

and _____

Next, click **Audio** > **Sound Blaster Audigy** > **Sound Blaster Audigy Platinum**. This takes you to the next page where you can choose your operating system.

Step 9

Under select your operating system, use the drop-down box to scroll down to and click **Windows 2000**.

What are the three different operating systems that are supported with this driver?

_____, _____, and

_____

Step 10

Under the section Drivers, find and click **ADGXPDrvUpdate.exe**. A new window appears that gives you information on the driver. To download it, click **Download** near the bottom of your screen.

Step 11

Read the statement and click **I Agree** to continue. It now asks where you would like to save the file. Click **Save**, navigate to your desktop, and click **Save** again. This saves it to your desktop.

Step 12

After the driver downloads, open the file, which starts the setup process. You can now delete the update you just downloaded if your system does not use the specified driver.

Note: This is only meant to show you the basic process of updating your hardware on your server. Your system might or might not have the sound card stated in the previous lab. You will need to find out what hardware is installed in your machine and go to the manufacturer's website to download the hardware.

Troubleshooting

Using the correct driver is one of the most important steps when installing a device. For example, if you install a new sound card, but try to use drivers that are built for a sound card made by a different manufacturer, the device will most likely not work or will work improperly.

Also, using the latest driver is a good practice to follow. When installing a new device, it is recommended that you check the manufacturer's website for the latest drivers available for their product.

If you experience problems with your hardware devices, first verify that they are properly connected. If the problem still exists after verifying the connection, try restarting your machine. Essentially, rebooting the machine refreshes and reloads the hardware drivers. However, if the problem still exists, the driver might need to be updated. To update the driver, simply follow the steps outlined in this lab. The latest driver can usually be found on the manufacturer's website.

The same applies for the operating system. If a problem persists, you might need to update the operating system. You should update on a regular basis to ensure that your system can run with maximum efficiency.

Reflection

Did you have any problems downloading and installing the Microsoft update or the drivers for the Creative sound card? _____

If so, explain how you overcame the obstacle:

_____

_____

_____

Worksheet 13.4.2: Using TCP/IP Utilities

1. If the universal naming convention (UNC) path is known, the server can be reached as long as the connection is good. The following is the format to use:

   _____

2. TCP/IP tools that test connectivity to another machine and that determine the path that a packet takes to reach the destination include the following:

   a. _____

   b. _____

3. Ping stands for _____.

4. The first step in checking for a suspected connectivity problem is to _____ the host.

5. The term _____ refers to the amount of time that elapses between sending the Echo Request and receiving the Echo Reply.

6. This tool combines the features of ping with those of tracert and provides additional information that is not displayed by either utility. With _____, it is possible to detect which routers are causing problems on the network and to measure how many packets are lost at a particular router.

7. _____ utilities discover the route taken by a packet to reach its destination.

8. Each operating system includes a utility to display the IP configuration being used by the system or network adapter. The following table lists the commands used by various operating systems. Fill in this chart:

Operating System	Configuration Display Command
NetWare	
Windows 2000	
Linux and UNIX	

9. These utilities display TCP/IP and NetBios statistical information:
   _____ and _____
   .

Worksheet 13.4.4: Windows 2000 Diagnostic Tools

1. What three basic functions does the Windows 2000 Server Task Manager monitor?

   _____

2. The Windows 2000 Computer Management snap-in contains several nodes that provide useful information about network configuration, what are they?

   _____

   _____

3. In Windows Task Manager, what is displayed with the Performance tab?

   _____

4. The general information of a network server, version of Windows installed, system name and type, and location of the Windows System Directory can be found under which tab in System Information?

   a. Software Environment
   b. Hardware Resource
   c. Applications
   d. System Summary
   e. Components

5. In Task Manager, what is displayed with the Process tab?

   _____

6. What is the purpose of the Device Manager?

   _____

   _____

   _____

7. If auditing is enabled in the Security Log, what can be audited?

   _____

   _____

8. The Hardware Resources tab in Computer Management displays what information?

   _____

   _____

   _____

9. This command runs a standard set of network tests and generates a report of the results. It is not a standard Windows 2000 Server installation and can be used without any flags.

    a. ipconfig

    b. tracert

    c. pathping

    d. netdiag

10. The command **C:\ > netstat –a** displays what information?

_____

11. What information does the **tracert** command give that the **ping** command does not?

_____

_____

12. The _____ command allows you to test communications between the current network server and another computer, and can use an IP address or an IP name.

13. What are the two different modes that can be used with **nslookup**?

_____

14. The _____ command displays protocol statistics and current TCP/IP connections using NBT (NetBIOS over TCP/IP).

15. What is the name of the TCP/IP utility that tests name resolution from a DNS server?

_____

16. What is the name of the TCP/IP utility that tests communications between the current network server and another server on the network?

_____

17. What is the name of the TCP/IP utility that reports the routers that a communication packet passes through when traveling from one network server to another?

_____

Worksheet 13.4.7: Server Shutdown

1. Can Linux send a broadcast message over the network? _____.

2. Can Windows 2000 Server send a broadcast message over the network?

   _____

3. What is the command to send a broadcast message?
   Linux: _____

   Windows 2000 Server: _____

4. What Linux command do you type if you want to shut down the server immediately?

   _____

5. What is the fastest, safest way to shut down Windows 2000 Server?

   _____

6. What are the Linux command switches you can use with the shutdown command?

   _____

7. What Linux command would you use if you wanted to send all users the message
   server shutting down at 4:00pm save all your work?

   _____

8. List the possible ways to shut down Windows 2000 Server?

   _____

9. Why must you inform users before shutting down the system?

   _____

10. Is this a valid Linux server shutdown? If not, what needs to be changed?

    ```
    /sbin/shutdown -r 15:00 server shutting down at 5:00am save all work
    ```
    _____

11. Type the syntax of a Microsoft 2000 Server shutdown in five minutes?

    C:\>

    _____

    _____

Worksheet 13.5.5: Redundancy

1. What is one way that you can help to cool a hot server?

_____

2. How do you make a network connection redundant in a server?

_____

3. How does the redundancy of a UPS differ from the multiple power supplies?

_____

4. What step should be considered if the data is extremely important?

_____

5. A _____ is a group of independent computers working together as a single system.

6. What are the two types of clustering models in the industry?

_____

7. What are two downsides to server clustering?

_____

8. _____ refers to how well a hardware or software system can adapt to increased demands.

9. To plan for scalability, how much extra capacity (minimum) should be built into the network?

_____

10. Give an example of how scalability works?

_____

_____

11. _____ is the designing and configuring of a server to provide the continuous use of critical data and applications.

12. List an environment that requires high availability.

_____

13. When planning for redundancy, what important factors should be considered?

_____

_____

_____

Worksheet 13.5.6: Hot Swapping

1. What is hot swapping also known as?

_____

2. What capabilities do hot swappable devices have?

_____

_____

3. Are there any disruptions to I/O requests and transactions on the system other than the failed component during a hot swap?

_____

4. What are some devices that are easily recognizable as hot swap devices?

_____

5. What is an example of a component that is frequently hot swapped in a server?

_____

6. When are warm swaps usually done?

_____

7. During a warm swap, do I/O requests stop?

_____

8. What is warm swapping?

_____

9. What is a hot spare?

_____

_____

10. Do hot spares contribute to normal system operation?

_____

Lab 14.1.8: Security Checklist

Estimated Time: 30 minutes

Objective

Upon completion of this lab, you analyze your school computer security policies. Based on you findings, you offer suggestions for improving the existing security policies.

Equipment

You need the following items to complete this lab:

- Pencil

Scenario

You have just been hired to do a review of the school security with emphasis on the computing environment. You have finished your initial procedures and are now going to review the computing environment.

Procedures

Answer the following questions to better assess your schools computer security.

Step 1

How are the premises protected against external intruders (guards, cameras, fences, secure parking area)?

_____

_____

_____

How is the building protected (security doors, locked/barred windows, building guards)?

_____

_____

_____

How is access to sensitive areas within the building maintained (keys, combination locks, proximity readers)?

_____

_____

_____

Who controls access to the sensitive areas of the building (facilities, security, IT)?

_____

Is a security alarm on the building? Is a separate alarm in the sensitive areas within the building?

_____

_____

How frequently is access to sensitive areas reviewed (monthly, semi-annually, annually, never)?

_____

Are key control/card control measures in place for departing employees?

_____

Are all production servers secured within a controlled access area?

_____

Are all production servers secured within a locked rack?

_____

Are the cases on all production servers locked, and is access to the keys controlled?

_____

Is removable media kept secured at all times? Where is this media secured (desk, locked cabinet, next to the server, offsite)?

_____

_____

How recently have the physical security measures been audited? Was it an internal or external audit? Were deficiencies revealed corrected?

_____

_____

If a card reader system is being used, how often is usage monitored? By whom?

_____

How easy is it to get on a computer connected to the network

_____

_____

Step 2

Did you find any problems with the computer environment security? If so, list what the problem was and what needs to be done to change it.

_____

_____

_____

_____

_____

_____

Troubleshooting

The IT department should be up to date on all security measures. The type of business dictates building accessibility and personnel access to the main office and sensitive equipment areas.

Reflection

Security is an important part of the computing world. Which companies do you think have stringent security measures in place?

_____

_____

Are your school's security measures sufficient? Explain your answer:

_____

_____

_____

Worksheet 14.1.9: Anti-Theft Devices for Hardware

1. What are removable media locks used for?

_____

2. Most high-end servers enable you to

_____

3. What is the motion alarm attached to a server used for?

_____

4. What are the four methods for ensuring the security of removable media?

_____

_____

_____

_____

5. What physical features should you look for in a server rack system to ensure good security?

_____

6. What is the advantage of removable drive locks?

_____

7. What is one of the most common security measures included as part of the server itself?

_____

8. What anti theft devices do server racks usually come with?

_____

9. What are the three types of add-on server security?

_____

10. What is another type of server case lock?

_____

11. In addition to built-in security, what other security measures are there for severs?

_____

12. The motion alarm is generally used in what type of environment?

_____

13. You have noticed that the server backup tapes for your department's server are stored in a cardboard box underneath the table that the server is on. Why is this a problem, and what should you do to correct it?

_____

_____

_____

_____

_____

_____

_____

Worksheet 14.2.7: Threats to Network Security

1. Common services such as _____ and _____ must be secured on a corporate network so that only authorized users have access to sensitive and personal information.

2. By the late 1990s, all the major developers of NOSs, including Apple and Novell, built their software around _____ and _____ services.

3. If you run TCP/IP services on a NOS connected to the Internet, you risk the following:

   a. _____

   b. _____

   c. _____

4. Several outside sources can be the cause of these attacks, including he following:

   a. _____

   b. _____

   c. _____

   d. _____

5. Describe the difference between a Hacker and a Cracker.

   _____

   _____

   _____

6. A _____ attack occurs when the targeted system cannot service legitimate network requests effectively because the system has become overloaded by illegitimate messages.

7. Denial of Service attacks come in many forms. Common DoS attacks try to take advantage of weaknesses with _____, or weaknesses in _____.

8. A _____ or _____ attack is designed to overwhelm the software running on the target system.

9. _____ attacks can be difficult to stop because they can originate from hundreds or even thousands of coordinated hosts.

10. A _____ is a program that presents itself as another program to obtain information.

Worksheet 14.3.5: Implementing Security Measures

1. _____ involves converting data into a form that cannot be easily understood by others.

2. When documents are encrypted on the disk, only a user who has the _____ can view them.

3. File encryption protects data stored on a disk but does not offer security for data because it is _____ .

4. IPSec uses two protocols: (Define both.)

   a. _____

   b. _____

5. SSL was developed by Netscape to provide security for its web browser. It uses _____ and _____ .

6. Popular e-mail protection programs include the following:

   a. _____

   b. _____

   c. _____

   d. _____

7. Public/Private Key Encryption is also referred to as _____ .

Notes

Notes

Notes

Notes

Notes

Notes

Notes

Notes

Notes

Notes

Notes

Notes